EATS, POOPS & HEAVES

First Published in Great Britain in 2011

Prion Books
An imprint of the
Carlton Publishing Group
20 Mortimer Street
London W1T3JW

Text copyright © 2011 Allison Vale
Layout and design © 2011 Carlton Books Ltd

A catalogue record for this book is available from the British Library

ISBN 978-1-85375-805-8

Printed in the UK by CPI Mackays, Chatham, ME5 8TD

10 9 8 7 6 5 4 3 2 1

EATS, POOPS & HEAVES

Over **1,000** Humorous Quotes on Babies and Babyhood

Allison Vale

PRION

CONTENTS

INTRODUCTION

Everyone will tell you that bringing a newborn into your home is as exhausting as it is elating. The coos and giggles and precious moments will, of course, go a long way towards softening the impact of the endless sleep deprivation, mountainous dirty laundry and the ubiquitous nappies. But there are days when it seems your little bundle of joy does little else but eat, poop and heave and if you're not careful your sense of humour can take as much of a battering as your pelvic floor.

Fear not! Help is at hand. With a little help from the questionable wisdom of A-lister mums and dads as well as some of the most hilariously irreverent comics on both sides of the Pond, this book is sure to put a titter back into your days.

From the urge to conceive, pregnancy testing, stretch marks and labour, to the many highs and lows of life with a newborn, this treasure trove of celebrity baby wit will keep you smiling every step of the way.

THAT TICKING CLOCK

Like a lot of women I got to my thirties and thought: I gotta have a baby now... while my mum's still young enough to look after it!

SHAPPI KHORSANDI

I decided I'm finally ready to have a baby. You know, for all the normal reasons, probably: I don't really feel like I have a purpose in life. I want someone to feel like they owe me something. What was the other one? Oh right, yeah, I have so much love to give.

ELLYN DANIELS

We're actually trying to have a baby now. I'm gonna tell him real soon... I'm just kidding – I'm not gonna tell him.

GINA BRILLON

I can't wait to become a mom. No question.

ALICIA KEYS

I found myself scratching around in the leftovers of my single male peers to find a partner with whom to have a child before it got too late.

ZOË LEWIS

playwright who had a baby by sperm donor

For the past 25 years, I've wanted to have a baby in five years.

CINDY CHUPACK
producer, *Sex and the City*

I guess the real reason that my wife and I had children is the same reason that Napoleon had for invading Russia: it seemed like a good idea at the time.

BILL COSBY

I've got a checklist of things I want – including a Brit, a Grammy, an Oscar and a white poodle. Sometimes it gets lonely, and I want a baby too! I'm ticking things off the list.

JOSS STONE

On weekends, I'd be thinking about going back to set on Monday just to see the baby.

VIN DIESEL
talking about *The Pacifier*

I visited those friends who'd just had a baby, and she was washing dishes and he was cleaning the house, and I burst with happiness. And in their minds, they were in this terrible domestic rut.

JOSH LUCAS

What good is it being Marilyn Monroe? Why can't I just be an ordinary woman? A woman who can have a family? I'd settle for just one baby. My own baby.

MARILYN MONROE

My girlfriends were having babies one by one, and I started to feel as if I was missing out on one of life's great experiences.

ZOË LEWIS

All I wanted to ever do was get married and have babies, have a house. So it's weird that I'm in a rock group.

GWEN STEFANI

MAKING A BABY

Most babies are products of drunken evenings
and lack of birth control.

ANNA FITZGERALD
My Sister's Keeper

After the show last year my lady and I – Camila – went back to
the hotel and conceived the little lady who is now our daughter.
I promise you me and Camila are going to try not to get so lucky
this year.

MATTHEW MCCONAUGHEY
addressing the Academy of Country Music Awards

Ovulation sex has about as much variation
as walking the picket line.

JOHN EISENDRATH

I'd wanna know the guy!

JENNIFER ANISTON
when asked if she would consider artificial insemination

It's never the right time to have kids, but it's always the right time
for screwing. God's not a dumbshit. He knows how it works.

JUSTIN HALPERN
Shit My Dad Says

Conceiving a child as a gay couple is considerably more
convoluted than it is for straight couples.

LISA CHOLODENKO
movie director

Now I'm in a repeater zone;
I just want to make babies and make records.

GWEN STEFANI

I still want more children after this one. I want a huge family
because I love children. I've got a huge house and I want to fill it
with kids.

VICTORIA BECKHAM

At this point, we're still trying not to,
but I can't wait to not try not to.

PINK
on her plans to start a family with husband Carey Hart

You build up to it, don't you?
You have that bit of a chat, and you go,
'Alright? How's it going?'
You get on an' that and then a little baby pops out.

KARL PILKINGTON

I'm not pregnant right now, but that can change tomorrow or
the next day or next week. That is out of my hands.

MICHELLE DUGGAR
open to the prospect of having a 20th child

It's the Easter bunny... I've never had sex.

MINNIE DRIVER

There's people making babies to my music. That's nice.

BARRY WHITE

This is the second most bizarre thing ever to happen to me.
The first was when I was sued by a woman who claimed she
became pregnant because she watched me on TV and I bent her
contraceptive coil.

URI GELLER

We have long passed the Victorian era when asterisks were
followed after a certain interval by a baby.

W. SOMERSET MAUGHAM

It was easy. I went to the clinic and got some frozen sperm.
I brought it home, defrosted it, inserted it, and...
and I'm pregnant.

MOLLIE
Look Who's Talking

My husband and I are either going to buy a dog or have a child.
We can't decide whether to ruin our carpet or ruin our lives.

RITA RUDNER

Women who miscalculate are called mothers.

ABIGAIL VAN BUREN

My ultimate fantasy is to lure a man to my bedroom, put a gun
to his head and say, 'Make babies or die'

RUBY WAX

He only has one ball and I have a lazy ovary. In what world does
that create a baby? It's like the Special Olympics of conception.

MIRANDA

Sex and the City

Someone once told me that children are like heroin.
You always want more.

SARAH JESSICA PARKER

I went to the doctor and I said, 'Look, why am I not pregnant?
I'm doing all the right things, you know? I've stopped drinking,
I'm taking vitamins and I'm putting a pillow under my bottom,
and all this.'
And he said, 'Are you having sexual intercourse on a regular basis?'
I said, 'I can't do everything!'

VICTORIA WOOD

It's quite crucial, this egg business, apparently, 'cos you only get
one egg a month. You know; like the war.

VICTORIA WOOD

Doctor says to a man, 'You're pregnant!'
The man says, 'How does a man get pregnant?'
The doctor says 'The usual way, a little wine, a little dinner...'

HENNY YOUNGMAN

I know women ready to cross the desert
on their knees to have a child.
If I had problems [with conceiving], I'd be one of them.

MONICA BELLUCI

[Getting pregnant] was generally something I was open to, but I
wasn't doing handstands and taking my temperature.
I was just not being careful because I thought it would take a
very long time because of my age. So yes, it was definitely like,
'Holy shit'.

BETHENNY FRANKEL

I love being pregnant, I love giving birth, I love being a mum.
The best gift that I've ever been given is Brooklyn. I just can't
wait to be a mum again.

VICTORIA BECKHAM

The one in the morning doesn't need to be anything special – you can just get on with it, even if I'm asleep; I won't mind.

STACEY

Gavin and Stacey
Stacey talks to Gavin about needing to have sex
twice a day in order to conceive

I was reading the financial times when I saw the headline FANNY MAE COLLAPSE. For a moment I thought Kerry Katona was pregnant again.

FRANKIE BOYLE

I thought you could get pregnant if you swam the backstroke in the same lane as a boy who'd just swum the butterfly.

VICTORIA WOOD

My wife and I have five children and the reason we have five children is we do not want six. And those we have we want to get out of the house, before we die.

BILL COSBY

My wife is allowed to pick the magic number...
as many as she wants to have.

MARK WAHLBERG

We used an anonymous sperm donor, which I know is very
fascinating to a lot of people... A couple of weeks ago, I was
with the baby, and this woman comes up to me and goes, 'Oh,
my God. He is so cute. Who do you think he looks like?'
I'm like, 'Your husband.'

JUDY GOLD

I don't bloody want any more – that's it!

ULRIKA JONSSON

It is now possible for a flight attendant to get a pilot pregnant.

RICHARD FERRIS

THE REAL TEST

That little pink plus sign is so unholy.

JUNO

Juno

I put the tests in a Ziploc bag and rushed to the train station to
pick him up after work. I handed him the bag, and he gave me a
high-five! He hugged me too, of course, but we were
so taken off guard.

JEN SCHEFFT

My life changed from the moment I saw that blue stripe on the
pregnancy test... I knew I couldn't have a fag or a drink.

SARAH COX

BAREFOOT & PREGNANT

Somewhere on this globe, every ten seconds, there is a woman giving birth to a child. She must be found and stopped.

SAM LEVINSON

My cousin Amber is 17, having a baby, and she did that pregnant chick thing I hate… She's like, 'Go ahead. Touch me.' I said, 'Sugar, haven't you been touched enough?'

LISA LANDRY

I do not like pregnant women in my workspace. They always complain. I have varicose veins, too. I have swollen ankles. I'm constantly hungry. Do you think my nipples don't get sore, too? Do you think I don't need to know the fastest way to the hospital?

STANLEY
The Office

One minute they're saying 'I'm pregnant', the next they're saying 'I'm too thin to get pregnant' – I can't keep up.

VICTORIA BECKHAM

He tricked me into marrying him. He told me he was pregnant.

CAROL LEIFER

Vendela…[looks] like a boa constrictor who just ate a baby goat.

MINSUN PARK
on pregnant supermodel Vendela Kirsebom

The government is planning to introduce a GCSE in parenting.
Sadly most of the pupils who'd benefit are busy
looking after their kids.

FRANKIE BOYLE

A KICK IN THE STOMACH

It kicked! I think the baby kicked! Oh, no, wait. Oh, no; the elastic on my underwear busted.

PHOEBE
Friends

Life is tough enough without having someone kick you from the inside.

RITA RUDNER

Let's face it, you're a foetus.
You're just happy you don't have gills any more!

ROSS
Friends

Every time we sing one of our songs he starts kicking as if to say, 'Shut up, I've heard enough'.

NATASHA HAMILTON
from Atomic Kitten

Feeling kicks for the first time has been pretty rad.

CHRISTINA APPLEGATE

BLOOMIN' MARVELLOUS?

I don't know what the pregnancy hormone is, but I wish I could bottle it and have it forever.

DANNI MINOGUE

The psychosis: if anyone's been pregnant you know exactly what I'm talking about. You kinda go a little cuckoo. Yelling for no reason. It's almost out of body.

CHRISTINA APPLEGATE

I have pregnancy brain, which I never realized was a thing but it is. I sort of feel like a koala bear, where I'm slightly stoned all the time.

ALYSON HANNIGAN

I sit down a lot on the assumption my ankles are swollen, but they're not. I'm overfeeding myself all the most sugary items in the cupboard, despite not having any cravings yet, and I'm already on the lookout for big pavlova-type clothes.

DENISE VAN OUTEN

You're stepping back from yourself and watching this insane monster in front of you that's you, and you want to stop her but she's funny to watch.

CHRISTINA APPLEGATE

I looked up the symptoms of pregnancy... moody, irritable, big bosoms... I've obviously been pregnant for 36 years.

VICTORIA WOOD

Any man who had to carry a child for nine months would cave in about a month or two.

JOHNNY DEPP

If pregnancy were a book they would cut the last two chapters.

NORA EPHRON

My pregnancy was amazing. I was happy that whole time, I felt good, I had energy, I was like Superwoman. I wish I could feel like that for the rest of my life, that's how fantastic it was.

HALLE BERRY

It takes nine months to have a baby,
no matter how many people you put on the job.

AMERICAN PROVERB

I was a pregnant vixen.

HEATHER LOCKLEAR

Today I vowed that I was going to wear flats, and then last second, I threw on some heels. I can't wait to sit down already!

KOURTNEY KARDASHIAN

You feel like a Buddha!

HEIDI KLUM

I didn't have a single bad moment. Really, it couldn't have been easier. I would do this professionally if only it paid better.

JODIE FOSTER

I'm not stupid, I'm just pregnant.

MINSUN PARK

My new fashion statement is the 'fat plumber meets rapper' look. Since I can't bear to wear anything around my bump, I wear my pants and skirts so low I'm constantly in danger of showing my butt cleavage.

MINSUN PARK

It takes a really long time to cook a human.

KERRY GODLIMAN

A pregnancy is a marvellous moment
that I would love to repeat and repeat.

PAZ VEGA

It's been so completely bizarre,
it's like *Invasion of the Body Snatchers*.

MINNIE DRIVER

We're in the third trimester and basically I'm just dodging
punches right now from my wife... She's completely over me and
over being pregnant.

MATT DAMON

It was boring being pregnant. God, they drag that out, don't they?

KERRY GODLIMAN

Far enough along to feel very cumbersome.

GWYNETH PALTROW
when asked how far along she was.

So my typical day is I get up in the morning and, you know, figure out which room I'm going to go take naps in.

CHRISTINA APPLEGATE

Ante-natal classes are run by liars.

VICTORIA WOOD

Being pregnant is an occupational hazard of being a wife.

QUEEN VICTORIA

MORNING SICKNESS

I don't know why they call it morning sickness.
I am sick morning, noon and night.

MINNIE DRIVER

I'm so ugly, my mother had morning sickness after I was born.

RODNEY DANGERFIELD

Did Catherine Zeta Jones ever vomit into her handbag while
overcome with morning sickness?

MINSUN PARK

E-G-G-S. Ugh. I can't even look at them. I have to detour in the
supermarket. They make me want to throw up.

MINNIE DRIVER

Making love in the morning got me through morning sickness. I
found I could be happy and throw up at the same time.

PAMELA ANDERSON

I take a sick bag wherever I go.

KIRSTY GALLACHER

I've thrown up in almost every limo that has
taken me out in the last week.

KENDRA WILKINSON

I go through the cheese aisle and I'm like,
'Noooo!' All the stinky ones!

ALI LARTER

The past few months have been a bit tough because I've been
sick and stuff, but now everything's fine, because I've discovered
soups are the cure to my morning sickness.

LILY ALLEN

I'm a safe vomiter. You can totally keep one hand on the wheel,
grab your Tupperware, and just [makes retching sound].

MINNIE DRIVER

CRAVINGS

I craved Indian food most of all, which is probably going to drive my baby crazy.

PARMINDER NAGRA

Everything, I'm craving everything. Besides avocados, just weird things at weird hours.

CHRISTINA APPLEGATE

Oh my God, candy! I had a huge craving for candy... I actually took a picture of myself with my big belly in a little lingerie top, surrounded by bowls of the candy I like.

CHRISTINA AGUILERA

I eat everything! I bake myself strawberry shortcakes and then I wake up at three in the morning and I eat them.

ALI LARTER

So where did these cravings come from? I concluded it's the baby ordering in. Prenatal takeout.

PAUL REISER
Babyhood

I crave ginger ale big-time. I didn't drink soda before and suddenly it was like, 'I need a ginger ale'.

ALYSON HANNIGAN

By far the most common craving of pregnant women is not to be pregnant.

PHYLLIS DILLER

It's funny because I used to love chocolate – I was such a chocolate lover until I got pregnant!

Victoria's Secret supermodel
ADRIANA LIMA

My most intense craving was a waffle with butter and syrup. Weirdest maybe a relish and mayo sandwich, but only once, thank God!

KOURTNEY KARDASHIAN

I'm mad about crispy bacon. But I can't stand red onion, tea or coffee.

KIRSTY GALLACHER

I like chip butties... butter a piece of bread, put your steak fries – they're the best – in it, ketchup, and then close it, chomp, and throw up!

MINNIE DRIVER

I could do with a great big cup of soup right now... I could have it for breakfast, lunch and dinner. I'm serious – I just can't get enough of it.

LILY ALLEN

In my first trimester I craved macaroni and cheese, which is why I'm fooling you by wearing black.

JENNA ELFMAN

A HEAVY LOAD:
PREGNANT BODIES

I've got a really big baby growing out of my stomach and, quite frankly, it looks like I've got one growing out of my bottom too.

FAY RIPLEY

[A pair of heels] offsets the impending growth of width.

CHRISTINA APPLEGATE

Do I look like I had 10 cheeseburgers or something?

ASHLEE SIMPSON

Every four weeks I go up a bra size... it's worth being pregnant just for the breasts.

NATASHA HAMILTON

I didn't have a baby bump, I had like a planet, with its own moon back here.

ANITA RENFROE

I swear my butt is pregnant too. I look like the Dancing Baby from *Ally McBeal*.

MINSUN PARK

My ass is as big as my stomach, so nothing really fits right.

CHRISTINA APPLEGATE

I'm ugly and fat!

JESSICA SIMPSON

not enjoying early pregnancy symptoms

The breasts go first and then the waist and then the butt.
Nobody ever tells you that you get a butt
when you get pregnant.

ELLE MACPHERSON

It's quite scary when you see these celeb women who snap back into
shape to a size 8-10. What women need to remember is that the
majority of us aren't like that... If I want a Kit Kat, I'll have one.

ZOE BALL

I hate thongs. Do you know they make a maternity thong? I
tried one on – I looked like a kangaroo in a sling-shot.

SHERRY DAVY

EATING FOR TWO

Do you know, my baby was so big, it treated my inside like a smorgasbord?

ABSOLUTELY FABULOUS

There comes a time when a woman needs to stop thinking about her looks and focus her energies on raising her children. This time comes at the moment of conception.

ASTRID ALAUDA

You don't even want to look in the mirror after you've had a baby, because your stomach is just hanging there like a Shar-Pei.

CINDY CRAWFORD

Having a baby takes so much from you. It's the most glorious thing you'll ever do, but the aftermath is not so glorious!

HALLE BERRY

It's a terrific trade-off. Maybe I don't have the time for pedicures any more, but who cares if my feet look bad? I'm happy.

JULIA ROBERTS

One of the reasons I think I've gained weight pretty quickly during my pregnancy is that I'm not exercising as much as I do normally... I can't.

PADMA LAKSHMI

Charlotte: What kind of diet book are you looking for?
Miranda: I don't know. Something with a title like 'How to Lose that Baby Fat by Sitting On Your Ass'.

SEX AND THE CITY

You've been a fantastic mother. You've let them ruin your figure. Your stomach is stretched beyond recognition, you've got tits down to your knees and for what, for God's sake?

PATSY
Absolutely Fabulous

When I got pregnant I told myself, "Hoorah! I'm not going to the gym, I'm not watching what I eat." I did do pregnancy yoga, but purely because I enjoyed it. However, my indulgence made me gain 4½ stone.

ZOE BALL

Pregnant women are going to get £120 to buy fruit and vegetables... People are going to start pretending to be pregnant and will end up hiring dwarves with potholing experience.

FRANKIE BOYLE

I worked out three times. Well, I went to the gym three times, but I only worked out two of the three times. One other time I used the bathroom.

TINA FEY

I cried during my last session. I was like, 'I can't breathe, I can't do this any more. What am I doing?' It was crazy.

GWEN STEFANI
talking about working out at 38 weeks pregnant

I was like: 'Oh, who gives a shit? I'll have another burger!'

CATHERINE ZETA JONES
talking about giving in to pregnancy cravings

I was still heavy eight months out! I got myself together for my kids, you know? They need to know what I really look like.

JENNIFER LOPEZ

BREAST IS BEST!

I even make Jordan look normal!

KERRY KATONA
on her breast size during pregnancy

My body felt so much more balanced out. Because I've always had a biscuit [her butt] and I've never had boobs, and so I finally felt like, 'Oh, this is how it's supposed to be!'

JENNIFER GARNER

My boobs got huge right away. They got so sore, that if anyone even brushed up near me, I would scream.

KOURTNEY KARDASHIAN

I have not been without a bra this entire pregnancy. I refuse. I'm not taking any chances. I'm determined to keep the puppies up!

REBECCA ROMIJN

I woke up one morning and it was like I had coconuts underneath a thin layer of skin and my husband was really excited about it.

AMANDA PEET

So I now have 10 pounds more than before – and most of them seem to be in my breasts! I'd love to keep the extra weight in this place!

EVA HERZIGOVA

I'm so happy. I can't ask for anything more... except big boobs. I've wanted Marilyn Monroe curves all my life.

NICOLE KIDMAN

I looked like a porn star.

AMANDA PEET

talking about how her chest grew during pregnancy

STRETCH MARKS

I have cellulite. I have stretch marks.
I feel intimidated by Victoria's Secret.

REESE WITHERSPOON

Even though some might consider them a flaw, I've learned to
love my stretch marks.

JESSICA ALBA

I don't mind my Caesarean scar, because it looks like a smile.

GERI HALLIWELL

I slather [anti-stretch mark oils] on – poor Lee, it must be like
sharing a bed with an oil slick.

DENISE VAN OUTEN

Think of stretch marks as pregnancy service stripes.

JOYCE ARMOR

I'll take the stretch marks. I'll take the sagging boobs. I'll take
the cellulite I can never get rid of.

JESSICA ALBA

IMPENDING DELIVERY

If you mention the idea of home birth to someone of an older generation, they're always instantly mistrustful. But that's just a generational thing, like racism and never indicating.

MILES JUPP

I think it's important for the guy to go to the maternity ward and find out if there's a plasma-screen TV in the room, if there's internet reception, cell phone reception… a mini-fridge is always important. Things like that.

KEVIN NEALON

I do it every year. I get my hair and nails done, I get a facial, I have a baby and then I go to the Emmys.

AMY POEHLER

Sex and curry? There's no prizes for guessing who might have come up with this theory! Men are sitting in pubs going, 'I can't believe we got away with that!'

MICHAEL MCINTYRE

We're told our baby should arrive on 1 October, but it could be two weeks either side. In other words, please allow 28 days for delivery.

PAUL KERENSA

Watching a baby being born is a little like watching a wet St. Bernard coming in through the cat door.

JEFF FOXWORTHY

I was actually in the delivery room when my sister had her baby, and if you ever get the chance to do that, don't! It's horrible!

JEN GRANT

My wife was in labour with our first child for 32 hours and I was faithful to her the whole time.

JONATHAN KATZ

The old system of having a baby was much better than the new system, the old system being characterized by the fact that the man didn't have to watch.

DAVE BARRY

I have tremendous respect for women after watching my wife give birth three times. I could never, ever raise a child to whom I gave birth. You know, because a newborn is about the size of a basketball, and if I had to expel a basketball from my body via a very restricted passageway, I would never want to see that basketball again. Not even on weekends.

JEFF STILSON

I realize why women die in childbirth – it's preferable.

SHERRY GLASER

I went over to my wife and kissed her ever so gently on the lips, and I said, 'I love you, very, very much dear. You just had a lizard'.

BILL COSBY

Ten and a half pound baby – I don't know if you've ever seen one of these but it's like you're looking at John Goodman but from far away.

TOMMY JOHNAGIN

You came out of your mom looking like shit. She thought you were beautiful. Don't know what scared me most, your looks or her judgment.

JUSTIN HALPERN
Shit My Dad Says

When the baby comes out it was like nine different colours. Like, great doc, my wife just had a bag of Skittles.

RICH PRAYTOR

In the first minutes of life they don't look like a baby. They're blue, you can see all of their veins, their head's all mashed out of shape. Like, you're expecting Gerber, you get Gollum.

MARK MOSELEY

My son was pissed. Like Eddie Murphy, when the doctor smacked him on the butt. 'Oh no, you did not just hit me on my ass'.

MARK MOSELEY

The baby came out, and they said, 'What is it, Dad?' And I had
no idea. I've seen women before; it looked nothing like this.
They're swollen in certain places. I said, 'I don't know what it is.
It's ours. We'll love it. We'll keep it. Don't put it back.'

MILT ABEL

I emerged from the womb, right, I was wearing a top hat and
I had a cane and said: 'Mother, that was an awkward and
embarrassing birth. You should be ashamed of yourself, dear.
Now pull your nightie down; that doctor looks salacious.'

RUSSELL BRAND

It was quite a difficult birth, though. I ripped. All the way round.
I've got some pictures!

HEIDI
The Smoking Room

It wasn't gory at all – I cut the cord and everything.
It was the realest tear I ever cried.

USHER

I sat there and watched like the helpless dumbass that every man
is in the delivery room.

MARK MOSELEY

You ask women, you know, 'How painful is it? What are we
talking about here?' And you don't get an answer, you get
anger... and it always starts with the melon.

DYLAN MORAN

Contractions have their own rhythm, right, so, we had to
find our own rhythm to be a little bit above or on top of the
contractions' rhythm. We had a good groove going.

MATTHEW MCCONAUGHEY

Why don't you try squeezing something the size of a watermelon
out of an opening the size of a lemon and see how hot YOU look?

MOLLIE
Look Who's Talking

Contractions aren't that bad. If you've ever had bad cramps,
that's what they're like.

JESSICA ALBA

I'm taping the delivery, you know, wrapped up in the miracle
of life, and suddenly Kelly starts swearing because the epidural
didn't work.

JOEY FATONE

Toward the end – no joke – I had full-on hallucinations in between pushing. It was crazy!

BUSY PHILIPPS

We found a great rhythm. Contractions started kicking in. I sat there with her, right between her legs. We got tribal on it, we danced to it! I was DJ-ing this Brazilian music.

MATTHEW MCCONAUGHEY

The whole thing was very surreal.

TIFFANI THEISSEN
on childbirth

Who knows? I'm an early riser. Maybe Bryn is too.

BETHENNY FRANKEL
on her premature labour

The scariest part of having a baby is eating the afterbirth. Luckily, it goes down well with a squeeze of lemon and some kosher salt.

LIDDA LANDRY

It feels like I'm shitting a knife!

ANGIE OSTROWISKI
She's Having a Baby

I hate you! You did this to me you miserable piece of dick-brained, horseshit, slime-sucking son of a whore bitch!

GAIL DWYER
Nine Months

Young Lorelai: Okay, this is a big pain and I'd really like it to go away, please.
Nurse: Just breathe deep, honey.
Young Lorelai: Breathing doesn't help, can I hit you instead?

THE GILMORE GIRLS

I think childbirth has been way too romanticized. You'll fart, poop, pee, and scream, all in front of ten complete strangers, all of whom are staring intently at your vagina, which, by the way, has an 80 per cent chance of tearing.

JD
Scrubs

What's all this fuss about fathers being present at the birth of their children? The way things are shaping, they'll be lucky to be present at the conception.

GEORGE H DAVIES

I'm not interested in being Wonder Woman in the delivery room.
Give me drugs.

MADONNA

You know when you welcome a child into the world, you witness
the birth of your child, and you've been there for that nine-month
period, you realise there's no doubt, there's no question that
women are the stronger of the sexes. There's no doubt.

JOHNNY DEPP

[It] was easier than having a tattoo.

NICOLE APPLETON

My obstetrician was so dumb that when I gave birth he forgot
to cut the cord. For a year that kid followed me around
everywhere. It was like having a dog on a leash.

JOAN RIVERS

I don't want to go through the pain. My Mom said giving birth
was the most excruciating thing she's ever gone through in her
whole life.

BRITNEY SPEARS

People are giving birth underwater now. They say it's less
traumatic for the baby because it's in water. But it's certainly
more traumatic for the other people in the pool.

ELAYNE BOOSLER

People say you look back and you remember the miracle. Fuck off! Two big salad tongs up my fanny!

JANEY GODLEY

You know where they put the sister? In a hard chair staring at your sister's vagina while she screams in pain!
To this day she thinks she gave me the greatest gift of all.

JEN GRANT

I basically got on a plane and was recovering [from a hangover] the whole way. He actually hung in there those last few hours. I think he was letting me sober up!

SCOTT WOLF

I think the key to having a baby naturally is being able to completely relax and get out of the way of your body's ability to get the job done.

KAITLIN OLSON
during her first pregnancy

Delivery is the wrong word... Delivery is 'Here's your pizza.'
Takes 30 minutes or less. Exorcism, I think, is more apt.

JEFF STILSON

If you're going to attend the birth always stay out of
punching range.

JEFF GREEN

I remember looking down at myself [during labour] thinking,
'There's a design fault here.'

VICTORIA WOOD

They've got this obsession now they want to show you the
baby's head coming out and they're always getting a mirror to
try and show you. It's just like being at the hairdresser's when
they show you the back of your head... You're thinking, 'Well, it
looks terrible, but it might be all right when I've run it under the
cold tap.'

VICTORIA WOOD

I don't want some scalpel-happy male doctor with no vested
interest in the equipment down there re-modelling... I just want
to gain a baby without losing traction.

SUSAN
Coupling

If the baby is too big the doctor has to chop your bottom off.

MORWENNA BANKS

Suddenly I'm realizing that there's a baby that's got to come out and someone is going to have to be there to push it out.

HALLE BERRY

I've only just managed to look at the pictures of the birth. I only looked at a few pictures and they do make you kind of go, 'Owwww! Ouch!' But then I look at him.
I want another one of them.

MINNIE DRIVER

They were trying to put the IV in me, and I began laughing so hard, with tears rolling down my face. I was out of my mind.

ANGELINA JOLIE

I was in bed watching South Park! I couldn't sleep because I had really bad acid reflux. I got up to go to the toilet and my waters broke. I Googled it and it said I probably wasn't in labour, so I got back into bed and watched a few more episodes.

CHANELLE HAYES

I'm really scared of the actual childbirth situation.

RIHANNA

Another thing they never tell you about having a baby: as the baby pops out the front, a haemorrhoid pops out the back. Mine was massive. Weighed more than the baby.

VICTORIA WOOD

The thing changed colours, like, five times!

BILL COSBY
on the birth of his first child

I think the sole reason for the man to be there [in the delivery room] is just so the woman has someone to scream obscenities at.

MARK MOSELEY

Do you know, I was so long in labour, they had to shave me twice?

ABSOLUTELY FABULOUS

Mum did most of the pushing and then towards the end enjoyed a wee bit of help from a very nice man called Pat. I think I may love him, I know Tash definitely does.

CHRIS EVANS

WHAT NOT TO SAY TO A WOMAN IN LABOUR

'Is that normal?' Even if you think your voice is completely devoid of fear. 'Is that normal?' Bad one.

DADDY CLAY

Confide all your fears in your partner. Share with her your aspirations for the kind of dad you want to be. Just not while she's pushing a baby out.

DADDY CLAY

I don't think you realise just how lucky you are; I wish men could experience the miracle of childbirth.

Do you think the baby will come before kick off?

That was the kids on the phone. Did you have anything planned for dinner?

Listen, babe, you really don't need an epidural. Just relax and enjoy the moment.

You sure you're done, 'cos your stomach still looks like there's another one in there?

Keep it up, love. I'm just gonna take a nap.

Wait one second while I check my email.

See, love, that contraction wasn't so bad.

While you're busy there, I'm going to go grab something to eat.

Do you mind if I go back to bed? Bang on the wall when you have a contraction and I'll keep track of them for you.

My mom said it really didn't hurt that much.

WHAT'S IN A NAME?

Our son's the coolest. We named him Owen 'cause that's what we figured we'll be doing for the rest of our lives.

TOM SIMMONDS

I could not imagine playing peek-a-boo with a baby named Marge.

ELLEN DEGENERES

You tell me, in the last five years, anybody who's been introduced to a baby named Larry. Bring me baby Larry. Show me a baby Glen. Who are we gonna borrow tools from in the future?

DWIGHT SLADE

You know what was really hard for me? Coming up with names for our children. I panic when I have to name a new document on my computer. Damn, everybody uses 'Miscellaneous.'

JEFF STILSON

I don't have any children, but if I had a baby I would have to name it so I'd buy a baby naming book. Or I would invite somebody over who had a cast on.

MITCH HEDBERG

If I had a kid, I'd give him a name that would make everyone would want to say his name. I'd call him Pizza-Pussy-Santa. I would! 'Cos everybody likes one of those things.

DAVE ATTELL

My son's name is Oliver Gosling which is really British sounding. It's kinda creepy. And he looks British 'cos he's only got three teeth.

MEGAN MOONEY

Nicki: What do you think of the name Noel?
Bill: I think it says 'Kick me and take my lunch money.'

BIG LOVE

Her name is Princess Tiaamii. Princess because she is our princess and Tiaamii was Pete's idea because it's taken from our mums' names.

KATIE PRICE

What really bothers me is when celebrities give their babies the dumbest names. I mean, we've got names out there like Sailor, Puma, Moon Unit, Audio Science. I mean, what were these people thinking?

RAK GOOLAB

Harry Baldwin, now that's a proper name!

PHILIP SCHOFIELD
on Holly Willoughby's son

Always end the name of your child with a vowel, so that when you yell, the name will carry.

BILL COSBY

We're gonna name all of our kids Mariah, no matter if they're boys or girls… Mariah No. 1, Boy Mariah, Man Mariah, Tall Mariah. It's gonna be a house full of people named Mariah.

NICK CANNON
married to Mariah Carey

Britney Spears says she plans to name her son London, because that's where her romance with Kevin Federline began. The couple were going to name the baby after where it was conceived, but it was too hard to say 'Olive Garden Bathroom Floor'.

DAVID SPADE
The Showbiz Show

You have to look up more of the foreign-looking names or name it Zuzu or something.

CHRISTINA APPLEGATE

We chose her middle name because when she's pulled over for speeding she can say, 'But officer, we're on the same side.'

PENN JILLETTE
on naming his newborn daughter 'Moxie Crime Fighter'

I want to meet them first. My brother was almost a Duncan, and he's Andrew now. I think it might have ruined his life more if he was a Duncan.

PETE WENTZ

President Stiller would be a great name.

BEN STILLER

Sometimes it works out perfectly. We have a local weatherman here in LA and his name is Dallas Rains, so that worked out for him.

ELLEN DEGENERES

Driver is kind of a hard name to put with a first name, particularly boys' names... My friend sent me an email saying I should call the baby Duncan Driver.

MINNIE DRIVER

I named my boy Miller Lyte because that's my favorite beer. And my little girl is named Margarita Olympia... I liked that beer too, even though they don't even make it any more.

ROOSTER MCCONAUGHEY

There's been a lot of fighting going on in my household over names. Frankie is very excited. She just wants to call [her sister] Turtle.

AMANDA PEET

That's a lot of pressure; you're naming somebody and it's for the rest of their lives.

ELLEN DEGENERES

I like Brooklyn as a name - it's quite different - but you couldn't do it all the time. It wouldn't work if you were somewhere like Moscow.

VICTORIA BECKHAM

It sounded so sweet, and it conjures such a lovely picture for me – you know, apples are so sweet and they're wholesome, and it's biblical – and I just thought it sounded so lovely and... clean.

GWYNETH PALTROW
on choosing 'Apple'

I had to have something that combats against the Flowers.

BRANDON FLOWERS
explaining why he named his son Gunner

My baby is not called Ickitt, Picket or Licket, thank you very much! Go pick on Apple, Satchel, and Moon Unit.

M.I.A.
blogging about flack received for calling her son Ikhyd

I think you should name all your babies 'Ellen'. You know, it's a thought. Don't feel the pressure. Only if you want to.

ELLEN DEGENERES
to an audience of pregnant women

We have a worry that he doesn't know his name because we have so many nicknames for him... Sky Walker, Walkman, Walk-a-do, Walkathon, Squirrel, Little Papa.

TAYE DIGGS

I wanted him to be called River because I wanted something always flowing, immortal. My husband said, 'There's no way we're going to call him River.' But my father's name is Reinoldo, so it's an homage to him. And it's like water.

GISELE BUNDCHEN

The first [kid] that comes out I'm naming him Hrrrrrrr. I think it's beautiful, it's feminine, but it's strong at the same time.

DANE COOK

SLEEPLESS NIGHTS

People who say they sleep like a baby usually don't have one.

LEO J. BURKE

Insomnia: A contagious disease often transmitted
from babies to parents.

SHANNON FIFE

I won't be suffering too many sleepless nights when the new
baby comes because Jools is brilliant about getting the kids into
a routine.

JAMIE OLIVER

Even nice things don't make you happy when you're tired. A guy
would turn up at the door with a nice bouquet of flowers for
a job I'd done and I'd just think 'Great, now I've got to find a
f***ing vase.'

JO BRAND

I am sleep-deprived, exhausted, overworked... I had no clue
what to expect. It was like raising an animal in the wild.

BETHENNY FRANKEL

I blame my kids. I'm so tired, too tired for a two-way or even, frankly, for a one-way.

DAN BUCATINSKY

Some days I feel like everyone in my world has plugged themselves into my kidneys. I'm so tired.

GWYNETH PALTROW

Back in the day I was up all hours clubbing. Now it's my baby keeping me awake.

DENISE VAN OUTEN

They never go to sleep and it's always about them. But whatever, you know? I don't care.

JOE ROGAN

Because their bones are growing they can only sleep in certain positions, obviously. The crucifix and the swastika tend to be the most popular.

DYLAN MORAN

You say, 'Bed time, bed time, bed time'; that's not what the child hears. What the child hears is, 'Lie down in the dark. For hours. Don't move.'

DYLAN MORAN

I thought my new Slumberland orthopaedic bed was going to be very comfortable when I bought it because the man in the shop said to me, 'On this bed, you'll sleep like a baby'. I didn't realise this would mean I'd wake up crying every five minutes and wet the bed four times a night.

JO BRAND

Waking up when you got a baby, you feel like you drank a bottle of whiskey the night before, except the shit's in someone else's pants.

JUSTIN HALPERN
Shit My Dad Says

The child is born it takes a look around and thinks, 'Well this isn't quite what I'd hoped for. These people are idiots... But I gotta make the best of it. I gotta maximise my resources. So the key thing is to stop these people having any more children.'

DYLAN MORAN

Tired is the new black.

AMY POEHLER

He's an impressive sleeper (thank God!) and I'm his biggest fan.

JENNA ELFMAN

FEEDING

When it's just me and the baby and he's head butting my chest looking for booby… I have to go, 'I've got boobies, but they're only for decoration', you know?

DAVE HUGHES

I found out early on that I could not hold my baby without a shirt and watch TV at the same time because it hurts.

CLETO RODRIGUEZ

You know you're providing a real service. After carrying around your boobs for so long, it's nice to know they have an actual purpose.

HELENA BONHAM-CARTER

If you can write your name in the mirror with breast milk, you might be a Mom.

KAREN MORGAN

Violet would be there on set, and I would feed her and then go back out. I was covered in blood and mud and dirt, and so her little sweet pink outfits would be caked in fake blood by the time she went home… you don't want to see that on a little one.

JENNIFER GARNER

I just can't stop losing weight with the breastfeeding. I ate as much as I possibly could, but kept losing. You'll see why when you meet Charlie.

JODIE FOSTER

Dean took a photo of me nursing, and I was horrified. I was thinking this poor baby must be so scared of this giant thing coming at him.

TORI SPELLING

It's like a tiger going crazy. The kid doesn't stop eating and sucking away. Those used to be for Pops. Not any more!

ADAM SANDLER

Right now she needs mom because all she does is eat. I have a feeling that when she starts talking she's going to be a daddy's girl.

JOEL MADDEN
husband to Nicole Richie

When you are nursing a small infant it literally sucks everything out of you!

JILL HENNESSY

One does become a Dairy Queen open 24 hours a day.

GABRIELLE REECE

We're like bartenders. We're like waiters.

ANGELINA JOLIE

There are three reasons for breast feeding: the milk is always at the right temperature; it comes in attractive containers; and the cat can't get it.

IRENA CHALMERS

Mum has moved on from producing semi-skimmed to the full-fat version of Noah's food and as a result experienced the "milk shakes" for most of the night.

CHRIS EVANS

I'm sure if he could breast-feed, he would have.

CATHERINE ZETA JONES
on Michael Douglas

She ate everything that I ate, through my breast milk. My baby was having a little bit of yak, a little bit of curry goat, a little bit of duck balls.

PADMA LAKSHMI

I'm not trying to be insensitive, your baby needs to eat, but so do I. If I'm at Applebee's, I'm already a little nauseous. Let's not add to it!

BILL MAHER

It would be so cool if I could breast-feed.

ALAN GARNER
The Hangover

If they can crawl up and reach for it, perhaps it's time to move on.

HELENA BONHAM CARTER

Some people here [in the US] think they don't have to breastfeed, and I think 'Are you going to give chemical food to your child when they are so little?'

GISELE BUNDCHEN

My theory is that nursing gives you superhuman powers. How else could I be doing all this when I'm usually a sleepaholic?

GWEN STEFANI

I always wondered why babies spend so much time sucking their thumbs. Then I tasted baby food.

ROBERT ORBEN

There is no finer investment for any community than putting milk into babies.

WINSTON CHURCHILL

He's 16 months old and he eats soap and paper. What's going on with kids?

CELINE DION

There are times when parenthood seems nothing but feeding the mouth that bites you.

PETER DE VRIES

My mother never breast-fed me. She told me she liked me as a friend.

RODNEY DANGERFIELD

An ounce of breast milk is even more potent than the finest tequila.

TORI AMOS

Our next presenter is the first woman to ever breast-feed an Apple: Gwyneth Paltrow

CHRIS ROCK

A thousand years ago the water supply in a Viking town would get contaminated so they would give children as young as three beer so they didn't have to drink the water. That's not good – you'd have to get a hangover. Imagine you're three and you're calling to your mate and he's three as well. And he's just sitting there, in dark glasses, sweat pumping out of him. 'Jaysus, I'm dying'.

NEIL DELAMERE

Then the milk comes in! Tons of it! It's like Marks and Spencers before a Bank Holiday.

VICTORIA WOOD

Children In Need... When was the last time you saw a child who wasn't in need? When was the last time a child said to you, 'Actually, that's enough raspberry tart for me, thanks'?

DYLAN MORAN

Anyone who says 'Easy as taking candy from a baby' has never tried it.

ANON

My mother's menu consisted of two choices: take it or leave it.

BUDDY HACKETT

Trying to breast-feed gave me such a creepy feeling. It made me feel sick.

DAVINIA TAYLOR

Your bosoms have gone into overdrive; people are ducking past you as if you're a lawn sprinkler.

VICTORIA WOOD

Carlos: Hey, Gabby, aren't we breast-feeding?
Gabrielle: Oh, honey, if you could swing that one,
more power to ya.

DESPERATE HOUSEWIVES

He wishes he could do more, but unfortunately the 'dairy queen'
here is the only one making the milk!

ELISABETH HASSELBECK

Ask your child what he wants for dinner only if he's buying.

FRAN LEBOWITZ

My sister had a baby. We could have company over and she'll be
there with her breast out, feeding him... cereal, or whatever.

EMO PHILIPS

When she was six months old I would overfeed her...
When they're really full they don't wake up hungry.
That sounds abusive!

JESSICA ALBA

It's awkward because at night the baby will sleep with us and my wife will leave in the middle of the night right after the breastfeeding and the baby's still hungry and she'll roll over and just look at me. I'm like, 'No, no. These don't function.'

KEVIN JAMES

I don't want a baby drinking from me – the thought of it makes me feel really funny. I think only a certain person could handle my knockers.

KATIE PRICE

My only input to those feedings is when I wake up and say, 'Oh you're a good mother,' and I go back to sleep.

DAVE HUGHES

NAPPY DAYS

Spread the diaper in the position of the diamond with you at bat. Then fold second base down to home and set the baby on the pitcher's mound. Put first base and third together, bring up home plate and pin the three together. Of course, in case of rain, you gotta call the game and start all over again.

JIMMY PIERSAL

Diaper backward spells repaid. Think about it.

MARSHALL MCLUHAN

Honestly, my favourite thing is when they're just wearing diapers. I think that's when they look the best!

GWEN STEFANI

I change a diaper with the best of them. Guys know, we time it! We're like, 'Oh, you want us to do it? How fast do you do it in?' Girls are like, 'Uhh, I don't know.' Guys are like, 'Forty-six seconds!'

FREDDIE PRINZE JR

Men should always change diapers. It's a very rewarding experience. It's mentally cleansing. It's like washing dishes, but imagine if the dishes were your kids, so you really love the dishes.

CHRIS MARTIN

Laughter is like changing a baby's diaper. It doesn't permanently solve any problems, but it makes things more acceptable for a while.

ANON

I love the smell of diapers; I even like when they're wet and you smell them all warm like a baked good.

SARAH JESSICA PARKER

[Levi] gets the joke when he pees on me. He laughs. He laughs his butt off!

MATTHEW MCCONAUGHEY

Of course I do diapers. What do you take me for?

VIN DIESEL

I didn't realize changing diapers was going to be as fun... it's like, 'Let's change a diaper! I hope she's made a doodoo, so I can just change it.

JON HEDER

It is love. Let me tell you, his diapers are no joke. But even then I'm such a proud father I'm like, 'Good for you! Good for you, little man!'

TAYE DIGGS

When those directions on the side of the Pampers box say,
'Holds 6-12 pounds', they're not kidding!

JEFF FOXWORTHY

Changing a diaper is a lot like getting a present from your
grandmother - you're not sure what you've got but you're pretty
sure you're not going to like it.

JEFF FOXWORTHY

I think the baby shit... Well, I'm smelling shit right now, so if it
ain't the baby, one of you has a big f**king problem.

JUSTIN HALPERN
Shit My Dad Says

No one likes change but babies in diapers.

BARBARA JOHNSON

Usually the triumph of my day is, you know, everybody making
it to the potty.

JULIA ROBERTS

I started potty-training my son about a month ago. The Potty
Dance was a saving grace. Getting him to learn it was easy - he's
a big dancer.

TORI SPELLING

I love the smell of Balmex [diaper rash ointment]. Love it.

SARAH JESSICA PARKER

I'm impervious to poo, snot, urine, vomit. You can't get me.
You cannot break me down.

BRAD PITT

For me, the crystallizing moment was the night my kid pooped
up my back in our bed.

JOHANNA STEIN

Is this chocolate or poop? Is this chocolate or poop? [licks son's
hand and smiles] It's chocolate!

CAROLINE
She's Having A Baby

How can something so small create so much
of something so disgusting?

MICHAEL KELLAM
Three Men and a Baby

POO-POO HAPPENS!

BOB IRWIN

My mom put me in a Pampers commercial on TV.

CHRISTIAN SLATER

I refuse to do it. I let my wife do it.

WILL FERRELL

Changing baby is essentially a mechanical process.
Men approach it like a pit stop; they want it over
as quickly as possible.

CORRINNE SWEET

Oh, this is disgusting. It's all over and it's... It's sticky and...
We're going to need some kind of cleaning fluid to get this off.

PETER
Three Men and a Baby

I love everything she does. If she does a poop and I have to
change the diaper, I love that!

SALMA HAYEK

Having someone else to blame when there is a rude smell in the air.

JANE HORROCKS

I was toilet-trained at gunpoint.

BILLY BRAVER

One year, I'd completely lost my bearings trying to follow potty-training instruction from a psychiatric expert. I was stuck on step one, which stated without an atom of irony: 'Before you begin, remove all stubbornness from the child.'

MARY KAY BLAKELY

Like many other women, I could not understand why every man who ever changed a diaper has felt compelled to write a book about it.

BARBARA EHRENREICH

To be perfectly, brutally honest, those of us who are still carrying diapers everywhere we go are not at our most scintillating time of life...

LOUISE LAGUE

Most men cannot change a diaper without subsequently renting an airplane that trails a banner that says,
'I CHANGED A DIAPER.'

ANNA QUINDLEN

One of the most important things to remember about infant care is: don't change diapers in midstream.

ANON

You ever rinse out a baby's diaper in the toilet? Yuck.

EMO PHILIPS

I think I am [good at changing diapers]. I could have a race-off with some other dads out there.

MATTHEW MCCONAUGHEY

You have to change those diapers every day.

JEFF FOXWORTHY

YOU KNOW THERE'S A BABY
IN THE HOUSE WHEN...

You're never alone in the bathroom any more.

You find yourself cutting up your husband's dinner into tiny
pieces in restaurants.

It takes you two weeks to shave your legs: one leg per week.

You never go anywhere without a shoulder bag
weighing at least 15 pounds.

You find yourself rocking gently in a queue at the post office –
even though the baby's at home with your Mum.

You're almost back from dropping Little One at nursery before
you realise you've been singing along to the Barney CD in the
car all the way.

Carrying your little one around has given you bigger biceps than
you ever had from working out.

You refer to your mother as 'Grandma.'

You have no idea who's on Mad Men but you can name every one from In The Night Garden.

It takes you at least an hour and a half to leave the house.

You have trouble concealing a knowing smirk as you listen to a mum-to-be talking about how idyllic her routine will be once the baby arrives.

You absent-mindedly blow your friends a raspberry on the cheek instead of kissing them.

You stay on the line to cold callers - it's just so nice to engage in adult conversation.

You carry a ziplock bag of Cheerios at all times.

Your pelvic floor is a distant memory.

5am is when you wake up, not when you fall into bed.

ALL ANONYMOUS

MAKING THE
ANNOUNCEMENT

The wife is preggers and we've narrowed it down to me.

WOODY HARRELSON

Don't worry, Dave, it's not yours.

BRITNEY SPEARS

telling *Late Show* host David Letterman that she is pregnant
with her second child.

I think that's good news for both of us.

LETTERMAN

responding to Britney's announcement

I want you to sing so loud that the baby hears it.

GWEN STEFANI

announces her pregnancy to her fans
during a concert in Fort Lauderdale

Put it this way. We're going to need football boots.

LOUISE REDKNAPP

announcing the sex of her baby

I have the most lovely, healthy bouncing baby, she was all very
compact and the right size.

ANNA FRIEL

Sunnery and I are in the clouds. The critical first three months have gone well and I feel good.

DOUTZEN KROES
supermodel, expecting a baby with DJ Sunnery James

We're not dating and I'm not pregnant. We have not kissed or touched. We have not fought and broken up.

SANDRA BULLOCK
denying rumours about a relationship with Hugh Grant

Will you just have my baby, and let's just get it over?

KID ROCK
to Sheryl Crow while hosting the CMT awards

If it's a girl, maybe.

SHERYL CROW
responding to Kid Rock, having just adopted her second son

Rob and I are so excited it's stupid.

KAITLIN OLSON

She's just fat!

FELICITY HUFFMAN
squashing pregnancy rumours surrounding
Desperate Housewives co-star Eva Longoria Parker

I have a little penis inside of me!

ALI LARTER
announcing she was expecting a boy

I am pregnant!

ALANIS MORRISETTE
announcing her pregnancy in US Weekly's
'25 Things You Don't Know About Me'

Brooklyn was the first person I broke the news to after my doctor confirmed I was pregnant. Then I sent him over to David to tell him the secret.

VICTORIA BECKHAM

Thanks for the congrats on my foetus. No secrets here, just thought it would be fun to see how big I could get before someone noticed.

DIABLO CODY
screenwriter on *Juno*

She's a great lady to make a foetus with.

DAN MAURIO
husband of Diablo Cody

BABY TWEETS

This is what 7lbs 11oz of California dynamite looks like!

JIM CARREY
Tweeting about his new grandson

Having contractions now! Ooo-wee! It's like WHOA!

KIMORA LEE SIMMONS

Why does my baby ALWAYS fall asleep 5 minutes before we get
to where we're going?!? & why didn't I remember my book?!?

ALYSON HANNIGAN

Yes...yes.....YYYYEEESSS Baby Ethan is adorable,
perfect and scrumptious!!!

KYLIE MINOGUE

Nothing cuter than a 23-month-old boy. Even if he is covered in
chocolate and snot!

MELISSA JOAN HART

Ok so I did it, he's 7.8 pounds of the greatest stuff on earth...

KELIS

When I swaddle Bryn, aka chickpea, I call it 'burritoing' her.
Everything is about food. She looks like a tiny spring roll.

BETHENNEY FRANKEL

Am I pregnant again? I just ate Indian food for breakfast!

BETHENNEY FRANKEL

Headed in to see the ob. 18 week checkup! :) having to step on
the scale right after a cruise is cruel & unusual punishment.

NATALIE GRANT

Having the best time, have created a little nest in my bed,
endless feeding, cuddling, snoozing, snacking, nappies,
kisses & day-dreaming.

SARA COX

Woke up, 1st time I noticed my kids breath smells bad & her
feet smell like feet. What happened to the baby smell?
Growing up too fast.

SCOTT BAIO

I got 2 arms, 2 legs, a nickname, and I'm 2 inches long.
See y'all in October...

LANCE ARMSTRONG'S
Tweet from unborn baby #5

I'm now the size of a lemon, 3.5 inches long, and weigh 1.5
ounces. And oh yeah, I'm on Twitter.

LANCE ARMSTRONG'S
tweet from baby #5, a few days later

Up all night with the lil man again but I enjoy every min of it.
He almost peed in my face today.

KENDRA WILKINSON

Man it feels great reuniting with my best friend that I haven't
seen in 9 months... her name is COFFEE!!!!!!

KENDRA WILKINSON

Gearing up for a very hot and spicy curry night... yikes!

HOLLY WILLOUGHBY

Just had a baby boy. Hale, hearty and beautiful, born to Sunrise
by Soul Savers & Bonnie Prince Billy.

LAUREN LAVERNE,
tweeting the arrival of her son and the soundtrack for his birth

OMG it's my first time out after the baby and I've just left the
house and I'm crying. I hate going to the toilet and leaving him!

DANIELLE LLOYD

I was in labour for 3 of the longest most painful days of my
life. I don't understand when women say they don't remember
giving birth...
I will remember for the rest of my life.

KELIS

It's a baby boy guys! I'm shock, we're all very happy, mum was
amazing and both are well and happy x4 kids!! What?!

JAMIE OLIVER
tweeting about the birth of his first son, Buddy

TAKE IT FROM
SOMEONE WHO KNOWS

Your baby only needs a lot of light at night if he's reading
or he's entertaining guests.

LAWRENCE KUTNER

It sometimes happens, even in the best of families, that a baby
is born. This is not necessarily cause for alarm. The important
thing is to keep your wits about you and borrow some money.

ELINOR GOULDING SMITH

If one more person told me what I had to do when the baby
comes, I was going to shoot 'em.

KATE HUDSON

A parent's only as good as their dumbest kid. If one wins a
Nobel Prize but the other gets robbed by a hooker, you failed.

JUSTIN HALPERN
Shit My Dad Says

Did you know babies are nauseated by the smell of a clean shirt?

JEFF FOXWORTHY

Don't throw a baby at anything – even a burglar.

EUGENE MIRMAN

Hello, babies. Welcome to Earth...
There's only one rule that I know of, babies –
"God damn it, you've got to be kind."

KURT VONNEGUT

God Bless You, Mr Rosewater

If you spit on a Kleenex to wipe somebody's face off, and you don't think that's gross, you might be a Mom.

KAREN MORGAN

Some people have got advice, some people have got horror stories. I like people that look you in the eye with a glow and say, 'It's gonna be cool.'

RUSSELL CROWE

With kids, the days are long, but the years are short.

JOHN LEGUIZAMO

If you bungle raising your children, I don't think whatever else
you do matters very much.

JACKIE KENNEDY ONASSIS

Getting down on all fours and imitating a rhinoceros
stops babies from crying... I don't know why parents don't do
this more often.

P. J. O'ROURKE

This is annoying: friends of mine that haven't got kids but have
got a dog. And think it's the same.

KERRY GODLIMAN

A Harvard Medical School study has determined that rectal
thermometers are still the best way to tell a baby's temperature.
Plus, it really teaches the baby who's boss.

TINA FEY

Now the thing about having a baby – and I can't be the first
person to have noticed this – is that thereafter you have it.

JEAN KERR

The beauty of 'spacing' children many years apart lies in the fact that parents have time to learn the mistakes that were made with the older ones – which permits them to make exactly the opposite mistakes with the younger ones.

SYDNEY J. HARRIS

A characteristic of the normal child is he doesn't act that way very often.

ANON

You are worried about seeing him spend his early years in doing nothing. What! Is it nothing to be happy? Nothing to skip, play, and run around all day long?
Never in his life will he be so busy again.

JEAN-JACQUES ROUSSEAU
Emile

Never go to your high school reunion pregnant or they will think that is all you have done since you graduated.

ERMA BOMBECK

Children are unpredictable. You never know what inconsistency they're going to catch you in next.

FRANKLIN P. JONES

Parenthood is the passing of a baton, followed by a lifelong disagreement as to who dropped it.

ROBERT BRAULT

The one thing children wear out faster than shoes is parents.

JOHN J. PLOMP

Parenthood is a lot easier to get into than out of.

BRUCE LANSKY

Every baby needs a lap.

HENRY ROBIN

Having kids - the responsibility of rearing good, kind, ethical, responsible human beings - is the biggest job anyone can embark on. As with any risk, you have to take a leap of faith and ask lots of wonderful people for their help.

MARIA SHRIVER

One thing I've learned about children and antiques is that you just have to let go.

SHERYL CROW

The very best part of being a new mom is knowing I am kind of a f**k-up but I will always be a better parent than Britney.

LISA LANDRY

Dr. Spock does not just want to sell a book! Dr. Spock loves us!

MOLLIE

Look Who's Talking

I used to hear that song, 'I believe the children are our future ...'
and I used to think it was a trite song.
Now I realize it's a warning.

JON STEWART

You should never say anything to a woman that even remotely
suggests that you think she's pregnant unless you can see an
actual baby emerging from her at that moment.

DAVE BARRY

I think, at a child's birth, if a mother could ask a fairy
godmother to endow it with the most useful gift, that gift would
be curiosity.

ELEANOR ROOSEVELT

Youth is not a question of years: one is young or old from birth.

NATALIE CLIFFORD BARNEY

The one thing you've got to be prepared to do as a parent is not
to be liked from time to time.

EMMA THOMPSON

The only way for this father to be certain of bathroom privacy is to shave at the gas station.

BILL COSBY

Babies don't need fathers, but mothers do. Someone who is taking care of a baby needs to be taken care of.

AMY HECKERLING

The best way to get a puppy is to beg for a baby brother – and they'll settle for a puppy every time.

WINSTON PENDELTON

Hugs can do great amounts of good – especially for children.

PRINCESS DIANA

Children have never been very good at listening to their elders, but they have never failed to imitate them.

JAMES ARTHUR BALDWIN

Don't forget that compared to a grown up person every baby is a genius. Think of the capacity to learn! The freshness, the temperament, the will of a baby a few months old!

MAY SARTON

If you want your children to improve, let them overhear the nice things you say about them to others.

DR. HAIM GINOTT

When you put faith, hope and love together, you can raise positive kids in a negative world.

ZIG ZIGLAR

Children learn to smile from their parents.

SHINICHI SUZUKI

You will always be your child's favourite toy.

VICKI LANSKY

Children in a family are like flowers in a bouquet: there's always one determined to face in an opposite direction from the way the arranger desires.

MARCELENE COX

Our children are not going to be just 'our children' – they are going to be other people's husbands and wives and the parents of our grandchildren.

DR. MARY S. CALDERONE

There are only two things a child will share willingly – communicable diseases and his mother's age.

DR. BENJAMIN SPOCK

You have to let go of what you think you want. There'll be plenty of time for that later. Right now, go and be with that baby.

PAUL REISER

If evolution really works, how come mothers only have two hands?

MILTON BERLE

In automobile terms, the child supplies the power but the parents have to do the steering.

DR SPOCK

One thing they never tell you about child-raising is that for the rest of your life, at the drop of a hat, you are expected to know your child's name and how old he or she is.

ERMA BOMBECK

Never underestimate a child's ability to get into more trouble.

MARTIN MULL

Don't tell your kids you had an easy birth or they won't respect you. For years I used to wake up my daughter and say, 'Melissa you ripped me to shreds. Now go back to sleep.'

JOAN RIVERS

Kids. They're not easy. But there has to be some penalty for sex.

BILL MAHER

Children really brighten up a household – they never turn the lights off.

RALPH BUS

I've noticed that one thing about parents is that no matter what stage your child is in, the parents who have older children always tell you the next stage is worse.

DAVE BARRY

Never lend your car to anyone to whom you have given birth.

ERMA BOMBECK

Do not, on a rainy day, ask your child what he feels like doing, because I assure you that what he feels like doing, you won't feel like watching.

FRAN LEBOWITZ

Why do we find it necessary to be in the baby's face when we talk to it? The baby isn't happy about this encounter. You think the baby is thrilled about your nasty coffee breath in its face?

JUSTIN MCCLURE

Except that right side up is best, there is not much to learn about holding a baby.

HEYWOOD BROWN

The Golden Rule of raising babies: Lie. Lie to your mother, lie to your sisters and aunts, and above all, lie to all the other mothers you meet on the street.

ELINOR GOULDING SMITH

Women may give lip service to wanting husbands who take on an equal role in raising children, but many will pull rank when an important decision, like how to discipline or what baby-sitter to hire, has to be made.

PEPPER SCHWARTZ

I don't know any parents that look into the eyes of a newborn baby and say, "How can we screw this kid up?"

RUSSELL BISHOP

Fat moms are better than skinny moms.

ROSEANNE BARR

A child needs a role model, not a supermodel.

ASTRID ALAUDA

Guilt is to motherhood as grapes are to wine.

FAY WELDON

A CRYING SHAME

A crying baby is the best form of birth control.

CAROLE TABRON

The baby would cry and Vin [Diesel] would hold him and do all
these weird sounds and the baby would stop crying.

BRITTANY SNOW

Postpartum blues? Postpartum panic is more like it. We set out
to have a baby; what we get is a total take-over of our lives.

POLLY BERRIEN BERENDS

When Baby's cries grew hard to bear
I popped him in the Frigidaire.
I never would have done so if
I'd known that he'd be frozen stiff.

HENRY GRAHAM
L'Enfant Glacé

I would also like to point out that he, so far, is the only one of
the three of us not to have cried!

CHRIS EVANS
announcing the birth of his son Noah on his blog

Before you have kids, when you're on a plane and there's a screaming kid, all you can think is, 'Give me earplugs!' As soon as I became a mom, though, I got it. You find yourself asking, 'What can I do? You want me to hold him?'

MARISKA HARGITAY

We were on a family trip to Death Valley, and there were moments when my husband and I wanted to just leave the kids there – all the whining!

KELLI WILLIAMS

Adam and Eve had many advantages but the principal one was, they escaped teething.

MARK TWAIN

Promises are like crying babies in a theatre: they should be carried out at once.

NORMAN VINCENT PEALE

There is a reason babies cry... it's your halitosis.
Find some mouthwash.

JUSTIN MCCLURE

Since I had the baby I can't tolerate anything violent or sad. I saw the Matrix and I had my eyes closed through a lot of it, though I didn't need to. I would peek, and then think, 'Oh OK, I can see that.'

LISA KUDROW

If it's so hard to get pregnant, how do you account for the number of crying children on planes?

SAMANTHA
Sex And the City

Just being a mother is making me a big, weepy mess.

JESSICA ALBA

GETTING DRESSED
BEFORE LUNCHTIME

A baby's a full-time job for three adults. Nobody tells you that when you're pregnant, or you'd probably jump off a bridge.

ERICA JONG

I find it hard to get in the shower before noon.

BETHENNY FRANKEL

Baby wipes are needed because you don't always get to shower.

PAT O' KEEFE

After you have a baby, in a few months you work your way up to getting dressed. Then after a few more months, you can start doing your hair, maybe putting on make-up a few times. But you never, ever get back to accessorizing.

MICHELLE PFEIFFER

I would like to have a bath one day soon, and maybe pee.

SHARON STONE

WHAT ARE
LITTLE BOYS MADE OF?

Of all the animals, the boy is the most unmanageable.

PLATO

To be honest with you, I didn't care whether it was a boy or a
girl as long as it had a penis.

KEVIN NEALON

Five, five, five, five, one – yes, it's a boy!

DAN
Roseanne

And I came back into the room and saw James Wilkie combing
his hair down in a certain way and standing in front of the
mirror... I heard him say, 'I have to be handsome when I meet
my sisters.' It killed me.

SARAH JESSICA PARKER
on her son's uninhibited cuteness

It would be great to have a boy,
as I am in a totally oestrogen-filled house.

JAMIE OLIVER

My favourite thing about my son is that he comes home from school and the clothes go flying! Like, clothes off, right down to the undies!

KATE HUDSON

[My son] is at that age now where he's so loving and says the sweetest things to me. Of course, I still get karate chops and all those other sort of things, too.

LIV TYLER

Old ladies at bus stops wanna play the Guess the Gender game. They love that game. It's amazing to me that a game with a 50:50 outcome can evoke such speculation from old women.

KERRY GODLIMAN

Your sons weren't made to like you.
That's what grandchildren are for.

JANE SMILEY

My son laughs in his sleep. He must dream in slapstick.
It's awesome.

LISA LANDRY

SUGAR AND SPICE
AND ALL THINGS NICE...
LITTLE GIRLS

Honor is the best cure for stress.

JESSICA ALBA

Fame is rot; daughters are the thing.

JM BARRIE

They are the greatest curse of all great men, daughters.

JASON ZEBEHAZY

Girls are so much more advanced than boys... Like, they come out of the womb, talking: 'Are you my mother? Lovely to put a name to a face.'

MICHAEL MCINTYRE

I do think that little girl's toys are evil though... Like the Easy Bake oven – evil. Evil toy. Only three years old and already under pressure to bake a cake for thirty people with a bloody light-bulb.

SHERRY DAVY

When I was pregnant, I kept praying, 'Please give me a lovable and loving, mysterious daughter that I can be fascinated by.'

LEELEE SOBIESKI

It does seem weird that I don't have a girl. It's not up to me anyway, these things are miracles, so we'll see.

GWEN STEFANI

[Suri] likes to dress herself. If she wants to wear it, she wears it. I'm not going to tell her different. She's got great taste. She tells me what to wear!

TOM CRUISE

You have a girl. Unless I cut the wrong cord.

DR KOSEVICH
Nine Months

I really want her to be a girly girl and wear really pretty dresses. Then again, she'll probably rebel on me and become a DJ!

ZOE BALL

A BABY IS...

A child is a curly, dimpled lunatic.

RALPH WALDO EMERSON

Raising kids is part joy and part guerrilla warfare.

ED ASNER

A baby is a loud noise at one end and
no sense of responsibility at the other.

RONALD KNOX

Babies are such a nice way to start people.

DON HERROLD

Here we have a baby. It is composed of a bald head
and a pair of lungs.

EUGENE FIELD

Babies haven't any hair; old men's heads are just as bare.
Between the cradle and the grave lie a haircut and a shave.

SAMUEL HOFFENSTEIN

The finest of our precision watches, the most super-colossal of our super-cargo planes don't compare with a newborn baby in the number and ingenuity of coils and springs, in the flow and change of chemical solutions, in timing devices and interrelated parts that are irreplaceable.

CARL SANDBURG

I thought that babies were cute little helpless creatures. No! Babies are ruthless dictators!

DAVE HUGHES

DOUBLE – AND
TRIPLE – TROUBLE

It was just what, on a good day, I would describe as a happy accident (on a bad day, a cruel trick played by my almost rancid ovaries).

JACKIE CLUNES
on having triplets in her late thirties

There are two things in life for which we are never truly prepared: twins.

JOSH BILLINGS

Here's the cycle; they wake up, they cry, they go to the breast, they eat, they poo or pee, you change a diaper, and they go back to sleep.

PATRICK DEMPSEY
on his newborn twins

By 20 weeks I looked full-term. By week 30 I was hiring mobility scooters at Asda.

JACKIE CLUNES
on carrying triplets

My biceps are getting huge because I'm just lifting them both at the same time. I'm going to be Schwarzenegger by the time they're one!

JERRY O'CONNELL

[Tabitha and Marion] just turned four months old today! One would prefer to be held 24 hours a day, and the other is already suffering from type A issues.

SARAH JESSICA PARKER

I was much distressed by the next-door people who had twin babies and played the violin; but one of the babies died and the other has eaten the fiddle, so all is peace.

EDWARD LEAR

Two more Combs. Two! World, you're in trouble now.

SEAN 'P DIDDY' COMBS
announcing that he and model girlfriend
Kim Porter are expecting twins

Listen, everyone says to us, 'It gets better. It gets better.' That has not been my experience. It seems to be worse and worse.

JERRY O'CONNELL
on raising twin toddler girls

The woman who gave birth to octuplets in LA is surely the result of science gone mad. I've no objection to people being given a helping hand to have children, but it's cruel and unnatural to allow a woman to have sex with an octopus.

FRANKIE BOYLE

The children's grandfather says they are going into hiding so the media won't be able to find them. I think the 20ft buggy and the stink coming off their house as it tumbles down Nappy Mountain will be a bit of a giveaway.

FRANKIE BOYLE

I can't move any more... I'm a beached whale!

REBECCA ROMIJN
expecting twins

It's double the giggles and double the grins, and double the trouble if you're blessed with twins.

ANON

A good neighbour will babysit.
A great neighbour will babysit twins.

ANON

My wife and I were talking about splitting up but neither of us wants to take the children – that's our joke.

JERRY O'CONNELL
on raising twin toddler girls

You can spend too much time wondering which of identical twins is the more alike.

ROBERT BRAULT

When I have a kid, I want to put him in one of those strollers for twins, then run around the mall looking frantic.

STEVEN WRIGHT

When I was born the doctor took one look at my face, turned me over and said; 'Look, twins!'

RODNEY DANGERFIELD

With twins, reading aloud to them was the only chance I could get to sit down.

BEVERLY CLEARY

I wish I had a twin so I could know what I'd look like without plastic surgery.

JOAN RIVERS

We thought it might be fun to have twins.

SAM FRUSTACI

We have very much an 'After you' culture... Everything is 'After you'. Do you know the gestation period for Iranian twins in the womb is longer than anywhere else? You've got this mother pushing out twins. Two heads appear going, 'Please, after you!'

OMID DJALILI

I couldn't get upstairs, couldn't sit, couldn't stand, couldn't sleep... I felt as though I had a family of labradors sitting on my chest.

JACKIE CLUNES

WHO DO THEY TAKE AFTER?

I see myself in them, which is both good and bad.

USHER

She has my E.T. toes. They are so long!

BETHENNY FRANKEL

My little baby, looking up at me with his little Chinesey eyes and big fluffy hair that makes me know that he's mine. And his little black face that makes me doubt it.

MICHAEL MCINTYRE

Dave: I love red sauce, me.
Denise: I don't like it.
Barb: Ooh, it's funny that, isn't it? Him liking red sauce and you not liking red sauce, and yet you get on so well.
Denise: Yeah.
Barb: I wonder what sauce Baby David'll like.

THE ROYLE FAMILY

Did you ever notice that a new baby always seems to bear a striking resemblance to the relative who has the most money?

ROBERT PAUL

The baby is fine. The only problem is that he looks like Edward G. Robinson.

WOODY ALLEN

I have good-looking kids. Thank goodness my wife cheats on me.

RODNEY DANGERFIELD

I don't know whose child that is until it comes out and has a test. You shouldn't jump to conclusions.

EDDIE MURPHY
on Mel B's baby

God, they're all so much my husband. I guess when my daughter pouts, it's me!

JULIA ROBERTS

BABY IN DA HOUSE!

I now understand parents who have messy houses…
Now it's chaos, with baby-grows and bits of
half-eaten dinner everywhere.

ASHLEY JENSEN

A child enters your home and for the next twenty years makes
so much noise you can hardly stand it. The child departs, leaving
the house so silent you think you are going mad.

JOHN ANDREW HOLMES

Nobody tells you how all-consuming it is to be a mother – how
reading goes out the window and thinking too.

ERICA JONG

Baby-proofing. Why is this such a big deal now? Y'know, when I
was a kid it was like, 'Whoops! Joey fell down the stairs!' or, er,
'Whoops! Joey electrocuted himself again!'

JOEY
Friends

There's something comforting in a house full of kids. It surprises
me, because I usually like being alone, but I'm really loving it.

PATRICK DEMPSEY

I'm not someone who [lives] like, 'OK, this is a museum and you can't sit here and you can't touch this...' You come into our house and a giant elephant and lion are welcoming you. We have toys and things everywhere.

HEIDI KLUM

Now what we did is, we stopped paying the electric bill. That cuts down on any kind of shock problem.

KEVIN NEALON
on baby-proofing

We invited a neighbour of ours over who has an alcohol problem. We got her all liquored up, and we followed her around the house to see what she got hurt on, and then we fixed it.

KEVIN NEALON

Have you any idea how many kids it takes to turn off one light in the kitchen? Three. It takes one to say, 'What light?' and two more to say, 'I didn't turn it on'.

ERMA BOMBECK

A LIFE-CHANGING ARRIVAL

A baby changes your dinner party conversation
from politics to poops.

MAURICE JOHNSTONE

Our life has not changed; it just takes a little more prep time to
do whatever it is you're going to do.

MATTHEW MCCONAUGHEY

Before it happens, people who already have babies smugly tell
you it's 'harder than you ever imagine'. So to try and outwit
these people I adjusted my expectations to 'very hard'. But it
turns out it's even harder than THAT.

MARK WATSON

I don't remember what I did after 6:00, ever.

MARISSA JARET WINOKUR

My best birth control now is to leave the lights on.

JOAN RIVERS

Our sex life has been ruined since the arrival of our first baby.
We can't be so spontaneous because we don't want the nanny to
hear us. We can't scream and yell like we used to.

CINDY CRAWFORD

The last time I was looking at a mound of white powder on a
shiny surface, it was definitely cocaine.

MARTA RAVIN
TV producer

I don't wake up particularly early, my wife doesn't wake up
particularly early, but for some reason [for] our children, 5 a.m.
is their time.

JERRY O' CONNELL

Today I have a chance to join the human race for a few hours
– there are actual adults waiting for me with margaritas. Look;
I'm in a dress; I have make-up on.

LYNETTE
Desperate Housewives

I've never [been this organized]. Now I'm all about the schedule.
I think Joel's kind of annoyed about it. He's like, 'Stop talking
about the schedule!'

NICOLE RICHIE
on having a new baby

Only one woman's hands to feed the baby, answer the telephone, turn off the gas under the pot that is boiling over, soothe the older child who has broken a toy, and open both doors at once.

MARGARET MEAD

[My purse] is always filled with stuff I didn't put there, from leftover Tootsie Rolls to wet wipes that got squished to the bottom. It makes me laugh every day.

NIA VARDALOS

Between your spittle, your diapers, your spit-up and drool, you got your baby food, your wipes, your formula, your leaky bottles, sweaty baby backs, and numerous other untraceable sources – all creating an ever-present moistness in my life, which heretofore was mainly dry.

PAUL REISER

This little baby is like a Prozac raindrop from a thundercloud of depression.

ABSOLUTELY FABULOUS

PRECIOUS MOMENTS

The hot, moist smell of babies fresh from naps.

BARBARA LAZEAR ASCHER

If your baby is beautiful and perfect, never cries or fusses, sleeps on schedule and burps on demand, an angel all the time, you're the grandma.

THERESA BLOOMINGDALE

Having a child is surely the most beautifully irrational act that two people in love can commit.

BILL COSBY

There are moments when I feel like I have a long road ahead of me, with college and dating and driving and all of that.

GEENA DAVIS

It's an extraordinary feeling when your own child gives you a gummy grin because you've oinked like a pig at them (just at a time when [my wife] was starting to get a bit tired of it).

MARK WATSON

There is a sanctity involved with bringing a child into this world; it is better than bombing one out of it.

JAMES BALDWIN

I remember the first time Ripley saw her shadow. My God, it was like shadows had just been invented.

THANDIE NEWTON

My aunt [gave me the best advice]: 'Put her to sleep yourself every night. Sing to her and cradle her in your arms and sit by her side – every night. Because one day you won't be able to, and it's going to happen really fast.'

SALMA HAYEK

There is nothing you will regret more in your life – nothing – than not being present for your children.

JAMIE LEE CURTIS

The moment a child is born, the mother is also born. She never existed before. The woman existed, but the mother, never.

BHAGWAN SHREE RAJNEESH

He's magic to me; he breaks me all the way down.

USHER
about his baby son

The real magic wand is the child's own mind.

JOSÉ ORTEGA Y GASSET

No cowboy was ever faster on the draw than a grandparent pulling a baby picture out of a wallet.

ANON

We're boring; we never go out now! An ideal night in would be Norman in the front room; he sits there with his old records and puts her into the bouncer and I can't stand it, but she loves it!

ZOE BALL

If I heard myself talking a year ago, I'd be like, 'So boring!' But that's what happens. My baby is really fascinating to me.

LEELEE SOBIESKI

When a baby comes you can smell two things: the smell of flesh, which smells like chicken soup, and the smell of lilies.

CARLOS SANTANA

BABY TALK

My friend has a baby. I'm recording all the noises he makes so later I can ask him what he meant.

STEVEN WRIGHT

A baby first laughs at the age of four weeks. By that time his eyes focus well enough to see you clearly.

ANON

Ma-ma does everything for the baby, who responds by saying Da-da first.

MIGNON MCLAUGHLIN
The Second Neurotic's Notebook, 1966

The baby will talk when he talks; relax. It ain't like he knows the cure for cancer and he just ain't spitting it out.

JUSTIN HALPERN
Shit My Dad Says

Help! Help! Somebody burp me before I blow up!

MIKEY THE BABY
Look Who's Talking

You can't understand it until you experience the simple joy of the first time he points at a seagull and says, 'Duck!'

RUSSELL CROWE
on 17-month-old son Charles

You know it's a sad day when your child looks at you and asks, 'Daddy, are these organic?'

DYLAN MORAN

[My son's] only got two words: 'car' and 'map'. I'm slightly worried he's trying to escape. If his next word is 'passport' we are in serious trouble!

MICHAEL MCINTYRE

My husband is from Boston and I'm from Georgia and therefore our children are bilingual.

KAREN MORGAN

[My one-year-old son] is starting to talk now. He just calls everything a cat. He sees a dog, he's like, 'Cat'. He sees a squirrel: 'Cat!' He sees a brain scan using computerised axial tomography: 'Cat!'

DAVID PRYDE

Children ask better questions than adults. 'May I have a cookie?' 'Why is the sky blue?' and 'What does a cow say?' are far more likely to elicit a cheerful response than 'Where's your manuscript?' 'Why haven't you called?' and 'Who's your lawyer?'

FRAN LEBOWITZ

Children aren't really interested in your views on the world. You know, they have their own questions, like, 'What is the name for the spaces in between the bits that stick out on a comb?'

DYLAN MORAN

PLAYING DRESS-UP

My mother in Boston sent us a business suit – a little suit, a little man's suit… like he's got a job he's got to get dressed up for. Like he's gonna be leaving the house with a briefcase: 'No time for breakfast! Ah, jeez, I messed myself. Hold the car.'

JACK GALLAGHER

Nahla can't wear all the clothes I've bought, and we don't go anywhere because I can't deal with the paparazzi. Gabriel's always like, 'She doesn't even leave the house! Halle, you've got to stop'.

HALLE BERRY

I was with my wife and my baby at the supermarket and I didn't think. I just put my hat on Clara's head, because it was cold. And the looks! I couldn't figure out why I was getting death looks. And then I realized my 10-month-old baby's wearing a hat with the word 'Pervert' written on it.

EWAN MCGREGOR

Tell me this; why do baby clothes have pockets? That's brilliant. That creates images of a ten-week-old baby going, 'Wallet, keys, phone... let's go'

KERRY GODLIMAN

Suri has picked out her own clothes since she was one and a half. She says, 'I want this sleeve cut,' and it's like, 'OK, we'll cut it'

KATIE HOLMES

I try, but I'm not nailing the baby fashion. It's intimidating!

KATHERINE HEIGL

SHOPPING FOR BABY

They have a section called, 'New Baby.'
I don't think you need the word 'new.'

BRIAN REGAN

Have you seen the baby knapsack with the kid hanging in the
front? Could that possibly be safe? Yeah, that's good because
when you trip, you want a baby airbag to break your fall.

RUSS MENEAVE

Lots of my friends have babies. They all have those baby-
monitors so they can hear the baby from the other room, which
I consider a form of wiretapping.

STEVEN WRIGHT

I understand there's now an entire brand of buggy that has little
knives coming out of the wheels, like little Boadiceas, going
through Sainsbury's cutting old people off at the knees.

SUSAN MORRISON

If you put a baseball and other toys in front of a baby, he'll pick
up a baseball in preference to the others.

TRIS SPEAKER

TODDLERS AND TANTRUMS

A two-year old is kind of like having a blender, but you don't have a top for it.

JERRY SEINFELD

When my kids become wild and unruly, I use a nice, safe playpen. When they're finished, I climb out.

ERMA BOMBECK

When you're dying laughing because your three-year-old made a fart joke, it doesn't matter what else is going on.
That's real happiness.

GWYNETH PALTROW

Why don't I just put them back in me and cook 'em until they're civilized?

LYNETTE
Desperate Housewives

I've never met a two-year-old who is terrible...
I hope she's not looking at me thinking, Mom,
are the terrible thirties coming on with you?

KATIE HOLMES

Our daughter keeps saying that she's got little piggies [in her belly] and she has to eat brownies because the piggies need to eat brownies. And our four-year-old says he's got monkeys. So it's become fun in the house.

ANGELINA JOLIE

Children have a sense of style and purpose when they're walking around... and it's a great walk as well; it's not an adult sort of bemused shuffle. 'I'm going over here.' You say, 'Why are you going over here?' ''Cos I have a harmonica.' 'What are you doing with the harmonica?' 'I'm going to put it in the toilet.'

DYLAN MORAN

I swear, being on the road with a toddler's like being on the road with Guns 'n' Roses only minus the booze and the broads.

SHERRY DAVY

Yes, the toddlers run fast; they're all over the place! And the twins are always going in different directions at the same time. We've gated a lot of rooms in the house.

ANGELINA JOLIE

TOUGH LOVE

There are only so many ways you can say to a child, 'Please don't turn the light switch on and off... again. You have absolutely nailed down the principal finding of this experiment. When you turn it off, Daddy can't see anything. He stands on your toys trying to find you and kill you. And breaks his foot.'

DYLAN MORAN

My mom licked me – that was her punishment.

ROSARIO DAWSON
to Jay Leno

Were you a child that often required a lot of licking?

JAY LENO
in response to Rosario Dawson's revelation

I think I will be good when it comes to playtime. I don't know how good I'll do with the discipline.

JACK BLACK

Even very young children need to be informed about dying. Explain the concept of death very carefully to your child. This will make threatening him with it much more effective.

P. J. O'ROURKE

Madam, there's no such thing as a tough child; if you parboil them first for seven hours, they always come out tender.

WC FIELDS

Experts say you should never hit your children in anger. When is a good time? When you're feeling festive?

ROSEANNE BARR

Never raise your hands to your kids.
It leaves your groin unprotected.

RED BUTTONS

Discipline is a big thing for me too. I'm not raising no brat!

CHRISTINA AGUILERA

My mother said to me: 'When your father gets home, he's going to shoot you in the face with a bazooka! And I'm not going to stop him this time! He's always wanted to kill you! When you were born, he said, 'Kill it!'

BILLY CONNOLLY

In Britain they passed that law, you know? You're not allowed to physically educate your children any more. I was rather saddened, you know? I used to bound home from work to strike my children.

DYLAN MORAN

BABY SHOWERS
AND CHRISTENINGS

Your house is a medley of disgusting smells, there's nothing to eat, everybody's wearing bathrobes, there's no bar, I can't f**k anybody. Why am I here?

DYLAN MORAN

on single young men attending a baby shower

I'm giving a baby shower for my friend next week for 40 people and I started calling them yesterday. 'Can you come? Can you bring something? I don't know – a bagel?'

MARIA BELLO

The old Irish, when immersing a babe at baptism, left out the right arm so that it would remain pagan for good fighting.

BILLY CONNOLLY

I definitely want Brooklyn to be christened, but I don't know into what religion yet.

DAVID BECKHAM

My brother and his wife had a baby boy. They asked me to be the godfather...
So, they call you out there on the altar. They start firing questions at you: 'Do you reject Satan?'
'I do.'
'And all his works?'
'I'm not familiar with all his works, but I'm not a fan.'

TED ALEXANDRO

ADOPTION

If I could just have the thing and give it to you now, I totally would, but I'm guessing it looks probably like a sea-monkey right now and we should let it get a little cuter.

JUNO
Juno

I'm going to adopt. I can't handle doing that to my body.

JILLIAN MICHAELS

Everything's got to be even. Like, if I scratch this hand, I've got to scratch this hand. If I tie that shoe, I've got to tie that shoe. If a celebrity adopts a baby from a foreign country, I've got to kidnap an American baby, fly it to that country and drop it off in Namibia.

HOWARD KREMER

Me and Dot went in to adopt on account a' somethin' went wrong with my semen, and they said we had to wait five years for a healthy white baby. I said, 'Healthy white baby? Five years? What else you got?'

GLEN
Raising Arizona

Wyatt is definitely all mine. Little souls find their way to you whether they're from your womb or someone else's.

SHERYL CROW
about her adopted son

I want, like, four. Maybe I'll adopt 10. I want to have my own orphanage like Mother Teresa.

HEIDI MONTAG

I want to make at least another billion dollars before I adopt children so I can just focus on them: like, just move to an island and give them everything.

TILA TEQUILA

My mom and I joke about it when people say, 'You're just doing it because it's trendy.' My mom says 'Well, I'm trendier than everybody, because I was doing it in the 1970s when I adopted your sister.'

KATHERINE HEIGL

Jonathan Ross: Congratulations on your lovely little black baby.
Madonna: You might be going home with a black eye.

AT THE BRITISH COMEDY AWARDS 2006
following Madonna's adoption of her son David, from Malawi

I brought home a baby without telling [husband John McCain],
and he not only took it in stride but loved it.

CINDY MCCAIN
who adopted a baby girl from Bangladesh

You shoulda gone to China. You know, 'cause I hear they give
away babies like free iPods. You know they pretty much just put
them in those T-shirt guns and shoot them out at sporting events.

JUNO
Juno

For a very long time, I have had intentions to adopt...We're not
going to protect the Earth the way we need to protect it if we
don't stop making so many babies.

EVANGELINE LILLY

It seems people would rather children grew up in orphanages
than with famous white women. 'She may be sleeping in an
overcrowded dorm with no parental love but at least no one is
expecting her to eat sushi!'

FRANKIE BOYLE
on Madonna

We feel that there are so many kids who need adopting. We thought we'd do it after having a couple of our own, but we just changed our mind.

HUGH JACKMAN

When Slumdog Millionaire came out [at the Oscars] they were hoping the kids would fall off the stage so they could get them – take them home! Then she puts them in the basement and they make clothes.

JOAN RIVERS
on Brangelina

Adopted kids are such a pain –
you have to teach them how to look like you.

GILDA RADNER

Madonna has had her attempt to adopt a little girl from an orphanage disallowed. Sorry; isn't that the point of orphanages? To temporarily house children with the hope they will be adopted? It wasn't like she was wandering through Mothercare waiting to catch someone off guard.

FRANKIE BOYLE

The thing I want more than anything else? I want to have children. I used to feel for every child I had, I would adopt another.

MARILYN MONROE

On our last day at this orphanage a man handed me his baby and said, 'Would you take my son with you?' He knew, in Ireland, that his son would live, and that in Ethiopia, his son would die.

BONO

It's not like I want to hop on a bandwagon, because I said it 15 years ago – bringing a child into your life who is not genetically yours is one of the most beautiful things you can do.

TYRA BANKS

If I can't produce a boy I will have to adopt one.

JAMIE OLIVER

You should feel happy. I'm giving you and Vanessa the gift of life! Sweet, screaming, pooping life! And you don't even have to be there when it comes out all covered in, um…blood and guts.

JUNO
Juno

Mom said that what really cinched the deal was my smile. Once she saw that, she didn't want to look at any other babies.

GREG LOUGANIS
Olympic diver and adopted child

Somehow destiny comes into play. These children end up with you and you end up with them. It's something quite magical.

NICOLE KIDMAN

Maddox is my baby; he's by my side all the time, and I think I can give him so much. I can no more imagine living without him than not breathing.

ANGELINA JOLIE

A WORD FROM THE DADS

Having a baby changes the way you view your in-laws.
I love it when they come to visit now. They can hold the baby
and I can go out.

MATTHEW BRODERICK

Getting a burp out of your little thing is probably the greatest
satisfaction I've come across.

BRAD PITT

Babies R Us is the most emasculating place on the planet. I
mean, I walk in there and I get intense cramps in my vagina.

MICHAEL STEIN

You can just accidentally create human life but if you want to
build a shed, you have to really want to build a shed.

TOMMY JOHNAGIN

My baby looks like a Nazi. Even when he walks now, he's got this weird little lock-step thing going on. The hands are up for balance, I think, but it could be fascism-related.

DAVID PRYDE

A friend of mine called me because his little girl was born the day before [my son]. He goes, 'Who knows? Maybe they'll end up getting married.'
My little boy's a day old; his little girl's two days old. He's not gonna marry someone twice his age.

BRIAN KILEY

I have this picture of my daughter on my phone –
in the bathtub when she was, like, a year old. I showed this girl –
I'm in line at the store...The girl just looks at me, goes,
'Aw, is that your daughter?'
'No, no; I take naked baby photos. I gotta go. My windowless white van is double-parked outside, full of candy and teddy bears. I don't want them to melt.'

PETE DOMINICK

We had our first... on New Year's Eve. That's a rockin' birthday.
Kind of f**ks any New Year's plans I might have had for the rest of my life, but whatever; kids can be selfish.

JACOB SIROF

Your marriage goes to a whole new level. You not only fall in love with your wife in a new way, but you're forced to pull together. You have to become a united front.

HUGH JACKMAN

Once that baby hits, you go from being lovers to team-mates. It's like, 'Feed her. Pass her. Burp her. Pass her. Clean her. Pass her. Diaper. Pass her.' At the end of the night, we're too tired for sex. We just fall into bed and high-five.

MARK CRAIG TAYLOR

Joey: Ross, did you really read all these baby books?
Ross: Yup! You could plunk me down in the middle of any woman's uterus, no compass, and I can find my way out of there like that.

FRIENDS

The extra night's sleep in the hospital will be very nice because once we bring the baby home, if it's crying all night, one of us is going to have to take care of it. And I do not plan on helping unless it's a boy.

JIM
The Office

I'm the one who changes the diapers, the one that feeds them,
the one that bathes them, the one that puts them to sleep.

RICKY MARTIN

You get these scary mailings that says stuff like,
'Congratulations, new dad! Now, what about life insurance,
disability, college fund? What if they get sick, Dad? Think of the
future, Dad.'
So I did – I got a vasectomy.

MARK CRAIG TAYLOR

I spoke to Luca on the phone and he burped; I was in tears.

COLIN FIRTH

Make no doubt about it; my kid will dance. He might not dance
like I do. Regardless, he or she is still going to have a little rhythm.

MATTHEW MCCONAUGHEY

I'm not going to have a better day, a more magical moment, than
the first time I heard my daughter giggle.

SEAN PENN

I figure somewhere between kid number one and number seven,
I must have learned a few things.

MEL GIBSON

We've had bad luck with our kids – they've all grown up.

CHRISTOPHER MORLEY

Noah is officially the nuts. He is the coolest of baby dudes. There
is just something about him; he is, as Jonny says, a Zen baby.

CHRIS EVANS

Yes, lots of late nights... spent staring at the ceiling wishing I
had finished off on her tits!

FRANKIE BOYLE
on fatherhood

My wife said 'Rob, I'd love to have children.' Now, I'll be honest
– I wasn't sure. Did I want to go through it all again? The lifting,
the carrying, the mopping up of the spillages? And that's just
when you're making love trying to have the child.

ROB BRYDON

You can write a book, you can make a movie, you can paint a
painting, but having kids is really the most extraordinary thing I
have taken on.

BRAD PITT

Every day I'm proud to be a dad. When you have kids, there's no such thing as quality time. There's just time. Changing her diaper and her winning a contest – it's all good.

CHRIS ROCK

Kids take you outside your comfort level.

PATRICK DEMPSEY

Huck's going to get stuff I want; that's what's going to be funny. 'Look, Star Wars figures!' I know it's for ages four and up, but still, I will play with them until he's old enough.

BRAD PAISLEY

When you have kids, it takes the focus off of you. You forget about what clothes you're wearing, or if you went to the gym. It makes you a better person if you do it right.

JAMES DENTON

I would be the perfect one-parent family. I couldn't give birth, but I could give make-up tips and football tips.

EDDIE IZZARD

It's indescribable. You hold this newborn, and you realize you've got responsibilities like you've never had before.

TOM CRUISE

OK... OK... I'm an actor. I can do a father. Shouldn't be that hard.

JACK

Three Men and a Baby

A new father quickly learns that his child invariably comes to the bathroom at precisely the times when he's in there.

BILL COSBY

I've got young children and I have to lie about paintings a lot because their paintings are so shit.

SEAN LOCK

It's amazing – I'm bringing another life into the world. But at the same time, I'm like, 'Oh, crap, I'm responsible for another human being.' I don't even buy my own underwear; where am I going to find his?

NE-YO

The hardest job facing kids today is learning good manners without seeing any.

FRED ASTAIRE

She's been pregnant basically for more than half of the last five years and she's been nursing the other half, so I've definitely asked about as much as I can from my wife.

MATT DAMON

Having a baby dragged me, kicking and screaming, from the world of self-absorption.

PAUL REISER

At the same time that the experience is pulling you apart, it's also bonding you. You have this joint venture!

PAUL REISER

A man is not complete until he has seen the baby he has made.

SAMMY DAVIS JR

We're feeding our baby a healthy diet of Bob Marley, The Clash, Prince and, of course, No Doubt.

TONY KANAL
musician

When I take my children to the park they run in opposite directions and I have a split second to pick my favourite.

MICHAEL MCINTYRE

My father confused me. From the ages of one to seven, I thought my name was Jesus Christ!

BILL COSBY

It's not that he's being deliberately obtuse about the pregnancy, or that he's putting up a wall of denial – at least not consciously. It's just our natural male reaction to anything we don't understand. Men need manuals.

JON SMITH
The Bloke's Guide to Pregnancy

I haven't seen many 10ams before so I'm excited.

ALEX HORNE

[Children are] not like the ones I remember from growing up, you know? Being at parties and you'd do all the childhood things like running around and bleeding and torturing the weakest member of the group, you know? Simple childhood games.

DYLAN MORAN

My Dad knew I was going to be a comedian. When I was a baby he said, 'Is this a joke?'

KEN DODD

I've got seven kids; the three words you hear most around my house are: 'Hello', 'Goodbye', and 'I'm pregnant'.

DEAN MARTIN

I've got the brain of a four-year-old.
I'll bet he was glad to be rid of it.

GROUCHO MARX

Childhood is that wonderful time when all you need to do to
lose weight is take a bath.

RICHARD ZERA

I'm looking forward to seeing [the Edinburgh Fringe] through
my son's fresh eyes. I can't wait to watch him watching jugglers
juggling and dancers dance and be thrilled. He won't have seen
it all before. Even better, when we return next year, he won't
remember he's seen it all before either.

ALEX HORNE

The worst sensation I know of is getting up at night and
stepping on a toy train.

KIN HUBBARD

You make 'em; I amuse 'em.

DR THEODORE SEUSS

I married your mother because I wanted children. Imagine my
disappointment when you arrived.

GROUCHO MARX

I love kids. I was a kid myself, once.

TOM CRUISE

When I was born my father spent three weeks trying to find a loophole in my birth certificate.

JACKIE VERNON

I wish to thank my parents for making it all possible... and I wish to thank my children for making it necessary.

VICTOR BORGE

The place of the father in the modern suburban family is a very small one, particularly if he plays golf.

BERTRAND RUSSELL

I don't think my parents liked me.
They put a live teddy bear in my crib.

WOODY ALLEN

It's not easy to juggle a pregnant wife and a troubled child, but somehow I managed to fit in eight hours of TV a day.

DAN CASTELLANETA

I feel cheated never being able to know what it's like to get pregnant, carry a child and breast-feed.

DUSTIN HOFFMAN

It's a human being that you're responsible for. Scary, but even in its scariest moments it's fantastic.

WILL ARNETT

My daughter announced she doesn't believe in the tooth fairy. She was rummaging around in a drawer and found some of her old teeth… beside my wand and my tutu.

ARDAL O'HANLON

[Children] kind of disabuse you of the notion of your greatness pretty quickly.

MATT DAMON

I want to be my kids.

TOM CRUISE

My name has turned into Honey-Could-You-Just… 'Honey-Could-You-Just get me some tea? I'm changing his diaper.' 'Honey-Could-You-Just get the baby seat?' And it's always right when I'm about to sit down.

TAYE DIGGS

I got a hundred bucks says my baby beats Pete [Sampras]'s baby. I just think genetics are in my favour.

ANDRE AGASSI

One thing I do know about being a parent; you understand why your father was in a bad mood a lot.

ADAM SANDLER

Spank was really my first love – not that I didn't love my wife, but when he was born, it was like my first love was him. I never knew about those kinda feelings and shit before.

SNOOP DOG
talking about his first child, nicknamed Spank

I'm the goofiest dad ever – I'm doing backflips in front of him and spinning on my head and he's laughing at me.

USHER

He looks like a turnip, but a beautiful turnip.

COLIN FIRTH
on his infant son, Luca

I won't teach my children farts are funny; that would be the wrong thing to do. I'm not going to indoctrinate them with my own moronic sense of humour.

JACK DEE

I was actually smiling, talking to one of my colleagues about my new baby… It was nothing to do with politics.

GORDON BROWN
having to account for having been seen smiling

It's extraordinary to look into a baby's face and see a piece of your flesh and your spirit. It makes you realize you are a part of the human race.

LIAM NEESON

If the new American father feels bewildered and even defeated, let him take comfort from the fact that whatever he does in any fathering situation has a 50 percent chance of being right.

BILL COSBY

In our society leaving baby with Daddy is just one step above leaving the kids to be raised by wolves or apes.

AL ROKER

Each generation has been an education for us in different ways. The first child-with-bloody-nose was rushed to the emergency room. The fifth child-with-bloody-nose was told to go to the yard immediately and stop bleeding on the carpet.

ART LINKLETTER

A study has shown that the average Brit should have three friends. Oh, shit; looks like I'll have to have another child.

FRANKIE BOYLE

Desperately trying to come back down to earth today but having major trouble with re-entry.

CHRIS EVANS
after the birth of his son

CELEBRITY MUMS

Children do take over, but it's fantastic.

ULRIKA JONSSON

I'm going to go crazy; it's his first Christmas, so you have to go all-out... I kind of want to get him his own Santa Claus and just have like a toy store in the house, full of things.

JENNIFER HUDSON

I was stunned when I saw on the ultrasound a tiny, living creature spinning around in my womb. Tap-dancing, I think. Waving its tiny arms around and trying to suck its thumb. I could have sworn I heard it laughing.

MADONNA

When your kids come home, they don't necessarily want to talk to you. They just want to know you're standing there, ready to talk.

MERYL STREEP

She is just scrumptious! She was born a week early and I know it's impatient, but I'm really looking forward to her being a bit older and more awake!

ZOE BALL

Becoming a mom to me means you have accepted that for the next 16 years of your life, you will have a sticky purse.

NIA VARDALOS

I knew I was an unwanted baby when I saw that my bath toys were a toaster and a radio.

JOAN RIVERS

Sometimes, when I want to take on the world, I try to remember that it's just as important to sit down and ask my son how he's feeling.

ANGELINA JOLIE

Motherhood puts you in your place, because it really forces you to address the issues that you claim to believe in – and if you can't stand up to those principles when you're raising a child, forget it.

DIANE KEATON

One surprise of motherhood for me was how little control I have. It's been bittersweet and humbling to let her lead and to not try to be perfect myself.

AMANDA PEET

[My daughter is] very artistic, but she's also a perfectionist. I feel a little bad; that's the part I see in her that's like me – and you don't want them to have that at age five.

COURTNEY COX

I used to think, 'What if there's an interesting movie and it conflicts with the boys going to a new school for the first time?' Well, I didn't anticipate that was going to be about a two-second dilemma.

JODIE FOSTER

I try to call my mother, Betty, with more regularity because I think, 'What if Hazel didn't call me for two weeks?'

JULIA ROBERTS

I'm strict about manners. I think that kids have a horrible time with other people if they have bad manners.

EMMA THOMPSON

You know how parents rattle on to you about, 'Oh, you won't believe your life will never be the same', and you think, 'Why can't these people just get over it? All they're doing is yakking about their kids. It's such a bore.' And then you have kids and you just want to do the same thing.

UMA THURMAN

It's like a whole new dimension in emotion that I've never experienced.

GWYNETH PALTROW

I think it's important to share what I love – what makes me 'me' – with my son, so, I change diapers and I breastfeed him and I play with him and then I work. I want to show Max everything about me.

CHRISTINA AGUILERA

It toughens you up and makes you more pragmatic, yet at the same time it turns you into a bowl of mush.

CATE BLANCHETT

I am most grateful for my daughter Coco. That kid is unstoppable.

COURTNEY COX

I'm the disciplinarian; Guy's the spoiler. He's the fun guy. I'm doctor's appointments, lessons, homework. He's good cop; I'm bad cop.

MADONNA

When Princess is 18 and goes to be a Page 3 girl, I'd encourage her. I'll go: 'Yeah, get them out for the lads.'

KATIE PRICE

You know, I never felt like I was young at the time and obviously having Mia was absolutely planned… It's only now, when I meet people who are my age and single, [with] no kids, that I reflect and say, 'Bloody hell, I really have lived at a fast pace.'

KATE WINSLET

My child was not only carried by me, but by the universe.

CELINE DION

Of course I love my baby. I've got the original Beatrix Potter drawings. Look how much we spend on it. Look how much we care for it. I've even got Beatrix's remains buried in the garden.

BILL BAILEY
on celebrity mums

Seriously, the first thing this kid
is going to see when it's born is a football.

KENDRA WILKINSON

If my sons told me they wanted to be in the entertainment business, I'd lock them in their rooms until they turned 30.

BRITNEY SPEARS

I want my children to have all the things I couldn't afford. Then I want to move in with them.

PHYLLIS DILLER

Angelina has made pregnancy and motherhood fashionable.

SALLY LEE

Parenthood: the state of being better chaperoned
than you were before marriage.

MARCELENE COX

I used to be excellent. Since having a baby I couldn't tell you what day it is.

GWYNETH PALTROW

I didn't have any problem bonding with Honey, but I was plagued with insecurities about my ability to bring up my baby.

GAIL PORTER

When one of Lisa's baby teeth fell out here, the tooth fairy left her 50 cents. Another tooth fell out when she was with her father in Las Vegas, and that tooth fairy left her $5.

PRISCILLA PRESLEY

I've been chased through airports with a screaming baby because the photographers are ruthless, and they want the picture.

LISA MARIE PRESLEY

Motherhood is not for the faint-hearted.

DANIELLE STEEL

The baby clinic is always run by two hatchet-faced old boots who left the Foreign Legion because it was too free and easy.

VICTORIA WOOD

When my husband comes home, if the kids are still alive,
I figure I've done my job.

ROSEANNE BARR

He's my wonderful, precious, little Buddha.
He eats like a champion. He sleeps peacefully and he's the
apple of his daddy's eye.

SHARON STONE

And now it makes every day like Christmas. I can't wait to see
him in the morning. I can't wait for him to wake up.

KIRSTIE ALLEY

The Emmys for me this year was the Night of the Drunk Moms,
'cos I got a little liquored up... Amy Poehler who had had a
baby three weeks before and was like, 'I am OUT! Mommy is
out tonight!'

TINA FEY

I'll probably be a little bit hippie and a little bit Type A.

CHRISTINA APPLEGATE

discussing what kind of mother she anticipates being

One of the sweetest moments was when I overheard David on
the baby monitor kissing Brooklyn and saying, 'I'm the only
man in the world who can kiss you on the lips, because I'm your
daddy and I love you so much!'

VICTORIA BECKHAM

And another thing nobody tells you – or maybe they do tell you, maybe you just don't listen – is once you've got little children you can't go anywhere nice.

VICTORIA WOOD

The babies are amazing. They begin each day all warm and sleepy, smelling of promise.

JULIA ROBERTS

You feel like your heart has grown legs and arms, and that is your child.

MYLEENE KLASS

One is one and two is 20.

SHERYL CROW
after adopting a second baby

Since Betsy came along there have been moments I've been wiping up vomit or changing a nappy and pinched myself at the thought of how things have changed.

DENISE VAN OUTEN

I am very fulfilled in my home life, and what films do for me is to create an ironclad structure that, in my life as a mom, does not exist. It is a shapeless blob of happy chaos.

JULIA ROBERTS

Why is my hair starting to go as grey as Blake Carrington's? What is our local pub called? Are bootcut jeans still fashionable? These are just some of the questions I'll never answer now I've had my first baby.

MEL GIEDROYC
Going Ga Ga

Motherhood is not for everyone but it is for me.

SALMA HAYEK

My ideal situation would be to live on a farm in a solar-powered house with a hammock and a vegetable patch.

MIRANDA KERR
talking about her ideal place to raise a family

YUMMY MUMMIES

Yummy Mummy? That's just like a posh way of saying MILF!

SHAPPI KHORSANDI

As a working mother high heels don't really fit into my life any more – but in a totally wonderful way.

SARAH JESSICA PARKER

I did it for the Campari job. [The workouts] were horrible. I cried. And I haven't worked out since.

JESSICA ALBA
on getting back into shape after childbirth

When the baby cries in the middle of the night, you're gonna get up without saying one word. Doctors' appointments; you're driving. I'm not putting a car seat in my Maserati. And you will also be on bottle duty. That means washing, sterilizing and filling. That way I'll have some semblance of a life, and then maybe I won't hate you so much.

GABRIELLE
Desperate Housewives

If I were a single man, I might ask that mummy out. That's a good-looking mummy.

BILL CLINTON

OLDER MUMS & DADS

I want to have children and I know my time is running out. I want to have them while my parents are still young enough to take care of them.

RITA RUDNER

My mother's younger sister just gave birth to a baby at the age of 62. It's a miracle. The doctor said it could be a difficult delivery. He said it might even be dangerous – for him to look down there.

DAVID FELDMAN

I continue to stay young, right? I produce children; I stay young.

DONALD TRUMP

You're not meant to leave it too late. If you're thinking of doing that you're meant to put your eggs in a Tupperware box and stick them in the back of the fridge.

KERRY GODLIMAN

I'd rather be standing for my kid's high school graduation. I'm not looking to be rolled around.

MICHAEL DOUGLAS

I'm kind of torn because I'm a bit too old to have kids, but then again I think it would be important to have a lot of me's around in the future.

SIMON COWELL

A 66-year-old woman has become the oldest new mum in Britain after giving birth to a baby boy. She says the most important thing is that she is able to give the baby a normal, happy childhood. Which he will have. Right up until she dies.

FRANKIE BOYLE

My grandfather's 86 and he's having a baby.
Man, I hope when I'm 86 I can have babies.

ENRIQUE IGLESIAS

For me, there's a big difference between having a baby in your twenties and having a baby in your forties.

JANE KACZMAREK

They say that the reason my generation leave it later and later to have children is 'cos we don't wanna grow up I didn't realize how true this was until I told my oldest mate I was having a baby. She went, 'Oh, my God! Are you gonna keep it? Have you told your mum?'

KERRY GODLIMAN

I was actually in the school playground recently picking up my daughter and our local MP was there and she said to me, 'Oh, nice to see you. On Nan-duty, are you?' So I said, 'Oh, I've just pissed myself; can you take me to the toilet, Tessa?'

JO BRAND

Catherine Zeta Jones recently gave birth to a daughter. According to the Mirror, Michael was at his wife's side when she went into labour; he was in the next bed having his hip done.

MARTIN CLUNES

I might have a bit of IVF. I quite fancy being one of those 70-year-old ladies that has a baby, and then they push you round.

JO BRAND

I have a new focus that's outside myself, and that feels really good, in your forties, to have arrived at that place. I'm actually lucky and grateful that I waited until an age when I can really be present.

HALLE BERRY

I feel like a bit of a science experiment.

EMILY PROCTER

WORKING MUMS

I don't know how people do it. I was just at a photo shoot with Kate Winslet, and I was like, 'How the f**k do you do this? I don't understand.'
Kate said, 'I know; it doesn't work. Everyone falls apart. I haven't worked in 20 months.'

GWYNETH PALTROW

Work, come home, play, kid bounce, work again, go to bed.

TINA FEY

The funny thing about having children is that now I am twice as motivated to do a cool stunt because my kids will like it.

ANGELINA JOLIE

I didn't worry about leaving the fast lane – I was just so consumed with my baby that it seemed like the right thing to do.

SISSY SPACEK

I [balance work with raising two kids] with great precision. I plan everything in advance: who's picking up. We have charts, maps and lists on the fridge, all over the house. I sometimes feel like I'm with the CIA.

KATE WINSLET

Nobody puts Baby in a corner.

KATIE COURIC
on her motto for achieving a home/work balance

I had to get back to work [after Alice was born]. NBC had me under contract; the baby and I only had a verbal agreement.

TINA FEY

My biggest dilemma is getting home for bath time.

MARCIA CROSS

THINGS I DON'T LIKE
ABOUT BABIES

If you were to open up a baby's head – and I am not for a moment suggesting that you should – you would find nothing but an enormous drool gland.

DAVE BARRY

If you desire to drain to the dregs the fullest cup of scorn and hatred that a fellow-human being can pour out for you, let a young mother hear you call dear baby 'it'.

JEROME K JEROME

When you've seen a nude infant doing a backward somersault you know why clothing exists.

STEPHEN FRY

Babies have big heads and big eyes, and tiny little bodies with tiny little arms and legs. So did the aliens at Roswell! I rest my case.

WILLIAM SHATNER

People show you their babies on their phone now, and it's like a cashew with some hair coming out of it. The thing to say is, 'Nice phone'.

RICH HALL

A soiled baby with a neglected nose cannot be conscientiously regarded as a thing of beauty.

MARK TWAIN

My friends who have babies can't do anything. Having a baby is like a DUI from the Universe.

NATASHA LEGGERO

Let's not forget the three most puke-inducing words that mankind has ever thought of:
Baby On Board.

GEORGE CARLIN

I'm supposed to alter my driving habits because some woman forgot to put her diaphragm in?

GEORGE CARLIN

She has a soft spot in the top of her head. You can see her heart beating out of the top of her head. That's not cute; that's not finished!

TOM PAPA

Your brother brought his baby over this morning. He told me it could stand.
It couldn't stand for shit. Just sat there. Big let-down.

JUSTIN HALPERN
Shit My Dad Says

So this is a more delicate than glass, more precious than diamond, poop basket that you're handing me? It might vomit on my shirt but if I drop it, I'm the asshole?

JORDAN PEELE

The other thing creepy about newborns is that when you're holding them, half your brain is saying, 'Oh she's so cute!' and the other half is saying, 'Throw it!'

TOM PAPA

It's a shirtless, bald human being with a bag of its own crap around its waist.

PATTON OSWALT

My brother, Graham, was born six years after me. He was so beautiful, he looked as though he had been beamed down from Central Casting and I absolutely loathed him.

LORRAINE KELLY

Who cares? It's just going to be another screaming, whining, bratty little life-sucking poop machine.

DARLENE
Roseanne

In a couple of weeks' time, we'll be awoken by the cries of our own little bonny, bouncing Antichrist.

RODNEY

Only Fools and Horses

The worst feature of a new baby is its mother's singing.

KIN HUBBARD

I can't think why mothers love them.
All babies do is leak at both ends.

DOUGLAS FEAVER

Babies don't need a vacation but I still see them at the beach.

STEVEN WRIGHT

Even when freshly washed and relieved of all obvious confections, children tend to be sticky.

FRAN LEBOWITZ

It would seem that something which means poverty, disorder and violence every single day should be avoided entirely, but the desire to beget children is a natural urge.

PHYLLIS DILLER

Having babies is fun, but babies grow up into people.

COLONEL POTTER

M*A*S*H

Hearing people talk about their babies is often, as Aussie friends of ours say, boring as batshit.

MARK WATSON

Although they're extremely common, and pretty much everyone in history has been a baby apart from some obvious lifelong adults like Trevor McDonald and Moira Stewart, parents continue to drool over their own offspring as if they're the first people ever to procreate.

MARK WATSON

I'm terrified of babies.

LADY GAGA

Babies. All they do is eat, sleep and poop.

PETER

Three Men and a Baby

It's not a miracle if every nine months any yin-yang in the world can drop a litter of these mewling cabbages on our planet.

BILL HICKS

They're just all slimy and then they make weird goat noises... I might be thinking of a baby goat.

ELLEN DEGENERES

BABIES NOT WELCOME

My wife and I... we had a long talk recently. We decided we
don't wanna have kids. Then we decided we should have had
that talk before we had one.

JACOB SIROF

I can't imagine having a baby. You got this thing that runs after
you, and then it falls down, and then it falls into you, and then
vomits all over you. Then it wants to suck on your breasts.
That's like prom night.

LISA LANDRY

Envy the kangaroo. That pouch set-up is extraordinary. I'd have
a baby if it would develop in my handbag.

RITA RUDNER

I don't know if I want to do this all over again.

VICTORIA WOOD

I don't want to have a baby...
My genes are poisoned and I know that for a fact.

SARAH SILVERMAN

Do your kids a favour – don't have any.

ROBERT ORBEN

I'd make a horrible mother. I'd probably forget to pick the kid
up from therapy.

LISA LANDRY

Having a baby with him meant marrying that face for ever.

ERICA JONG

I had left home (like all Jewish girls) in order to eat pork and
take birth control pills.

ROSEANNE BARR

Children aren't the only things that bring you gratification and
happiness. That kind of change would have to be either very
well thought out, or a total mistake – a real oops!

CAMERON DIAZ

I hope I never have babies. That would kill me. Every minute I'd
be, 'Is the baby OK?' I'd worry too much.

HEIDI FLEISS

My womb is not yet beckoning for a child. I'm very far away
from that day. I'm also terrified it will ruin my creativity.

LADY GAGA

Obviously, it's not the right time for me to be a father, but the
one thing I haven't had the chance to do is be a great dad.

NICK LACHEY

We've begun to long for the pitter-patter of little feet – so we
bought a dog. Well, it's cheaper and you get more feet.

RITA RUDNER

I don't understand why anybody would want to shove a whole
human being out of their vagina... I don't care how many
generations of women have done it; that's f**king evil.

JANEY GODLEY

Love is all fun and games
until someone loses an eye or gets pregnant.

JIM COLE

I have nightmares about having children.

SHARON GLESS

I'm not pregnant! It's a miracle! I shagged and shagged and
shagged and all the little bastards missed!

JANE
Coupling

Well the pregnancy test said I'm not pregnant:
the hamster didn't turn blue.

ALICE
Vicar of Dibley

I don't have kids. My sister has two kids and the way she makes
it sound, it sounds pretty badass.

JOE ROGAN

Children are very, very over-sentimentalized really, aren't they?
The charities they have; they go on and on and on. Children in
Need of Another Biscuit.

DYLAN MORAN

For me, if I wake up in the morning, if I'm not on fire and I'm
not pregnant, I'm happy.

NANCY WITTER

I never met a kid I liked.

WC FIELDS

No wonder people are so horrible when they start life as children.

KINGSLEY AMIS

The trouble with children is that they're not returnable.

QUENTIN CRISP

What are they really, children? Midget drunks, that's what they are! People who greet you in the morning by kneeing you in the face.

DYLAN MORAN

Sometimes I see a baby and think: 'That's what I want: a baby.' Then I see a pair of shoes and I think, 'No, have the shoes instead.'

JENNY ÉCLAIR

Kids are wonderful, but I like mine barbecued.

BOB HOPE

Parents are the last people on earth who ought to have children.

SAMUEL BUTLER

Gabrielle: Before we got married we made a deal, remember?
No kids.
Carlos: Deals are meant to be renegotiated.
Gabrielle: We're not negotiating my uterus.

DESPERATE HOUSEWIVES

I love the idea of marriage and making babies – but not yet.
Not until I'm 30.
I basically chew my birth control tablets – I chew them like
vitamin C; I'm like, 'Nomnomnomnom.'

KATY PERRY

Of course we all wish we had a beautiful little baby to play with,
but when it comes right down to it, would I really want to give
up all those years of singing?

STEVIE NICKS

AN ABORTIVE EFFORT

Well, you know, I was thinking I'd just nip it in the bud, before it gets worse, because they were talking about it in health class, how pregnancy, it can often lead to... an infant.

JUNO
Juno

If men could get pregnant, abortion would be a sacrament.

ROSE F KENNEDY

Thank God for abortion. I don't mean to offend anyone but I wouldn't be a good mother. I shouldn't have kids.

HEIDI FLEISS

If there's a woman in leggings, eating chips with a fag in her mouth, sterilize her.

RICKY GERVAIS

What there is, is too many useless people.
Too many people who shouldn't have children.

RICKY GERVAIS

MOTHER ON THE EDGE!

The routine can kill me.

KATE HUDSON
about motherhood

Sometimes you just need a minute to say, 'I think I'm cracking', and just acknowledge it.

TINA FEY

When the kids were young and I was alone with all these babies, by Thursday I'd have a pity party, and John would walk in, see me hanging off the ceiling...

CINDY McCAIN
wife of Senator John McCain

Everyone should have kids.
They are the greatest joy in the world. But they are also terrorists. You'll realize this as soon as they are born, and they start using sleep deprivation to break you.

RAY ROMANO

Having a family is like
having a bowling alley installed in your head.

MARTIN MULL

Insanity is hereditary. You can get it from your children.

SAM LEVINSON

KEEPING PARENTS CLUELESS

I remember leaving the hospital, thinking,
'Wait; are they going to let me just walk off with him?
I don't know beans about babies!'

ANNE TYLER

It's quite scary that first night they leave you alone in the
hospital with your newborn child, because it takes them a while
to solidify.

SHAPPI KHORSANDI

Oh, don't be so stupid; smoke can't get in there, darling. Smoke
can't touch the baby. If it could you'd have come out looking
like prosciutto, believe me.

EDINA
Absolutely Fabulous

We're nowhere near mature enough to be parents. I'm positive
of that. After [our baby girl's] first feeding, she passed out, so we
wrote on her.

KP ANDERSON

I wanna bring my baby to a tanning salon,
like just to see what they do.

MEGAN MOONEY

Steve: I never bite heads off live foetuses.
Susan: Words never before uttered at a pregnancy convention.

COUPLING

I have a question.
Do you guys think it's OK to drink while you're pregnant if
you're planning on giving the baby up for adoption?

CHELSEA HANDLER

I'm only not smoking in front of Baby David until he's old
enough to get up and walk out of the room; then it's his choice.

DENISE

The Royle Family

I try to pick up and hold a baby every day, if possible, because it
nourishes me. It feeds my soul.

MICHAEL

The Office

It's a known fact that women love babies, all right? Women love
guys who love babies. It's that whole sensitive thing. Quick; aim
him at that pack of babes over there.

JOEY

Friends

I think having a baby's a huge responsibility. It's like a five-year commitment and you need to be ready for it.

CHELSEA HANDLER

I don't have a kid, but I think that I would be a good father, especially if my baby liked to go out drinking.

EUGENE MIRMAN

I just looked at her and said, 'Chelsea, you've never been a baby before, and I've never been a mother before, and we're just going to have to help each other get through this.'

HILLARY CLINTON

Babies are drawn to me,
and I think it's because they see me as one of them,
but... cooler, and with my life put together a little bit more.

MICHAEL
The Office

Social worker: Vicky, where is the baby?
Vicky: Swapped it for a Westlife CD.
Social worker: How could you do such a thing?
Vicky Pollard: I know; they're rubbish.

LITTLE BRITAIN

Stan: It's every man's right to have babies if he wants them.

Reg: But... you can't HAVE babies!

Stan: Don't you oppress me!

Reg: I'm not oppressing you, Stan. You haven't got a womb!
Where's the foetus gonna gestate? You gonna keep it in a box?

THE LIFE OF BRIAN

I'm gone a lot from home... and that's hard, to be gone three
and a half weeks 'cause then I have to ask my friends, 'Would
you mind going to the house and watering the plants, and turn
some lights on and make it look like somebody's home, and
make sure that the mobile over the crib isn't tangled or the
baby's gonna get bored?'

ELLEN DEGENERES

What am I doing having a kid? Like last week, I was gathering
all my roaches and consolidating them into one joint and now
I'm a parent?

JOHANNA STEIN

My sister's expecting a baby, and I don't know if I'm going to be
an uncle or an aunt.

CHUCK NEVITT

I did it with my dad. We're country.

BRITNEY SPEARS
explaining in part why she drove with son Sean Preston on her lap

Now look. There is nothing in the world to get uptight about.
We are two summa cum laudes. We can handle one little baby
for eight hours.

JC WIATT
Baby Boom

He was really good at babies; he could do that thing where he
could put the baby under his arm and open doors. I had to hold
her in front of me and go backwards.

JANEY GODLEY

I watched him grow up but, you know, you dangle a baby over a
balcony and that's it for me.

CHER
on Michael Jackson

So Carol, you're a housewife and mother.
And have you got any children?

MICHAEL BARRYMORE